Table of Contents

Table of Contents continued

Table of Contents *continued*

Introduction

The National Council of Teachers of English and the International Reading Association prepared standards for the English language arts. These standards "grew out of current research and theory about how students learn—in particular, how they learn language." These standards address "what students should know and be able to do in the English language arts."

One standard is that students should be able to communicate effectively by learning the "language of wider communication," the forms of the English language that are most commonly identified as standard English. Students must recognize the importance of audience when they write and speak so they will be able to use the appropriate form of language for the intended audience. The standards acknowledge that "students need guidance and practice to develop their skills in academic writing. . . . They need to understand the varying demands of different kinds of writing tasks and to recognize how to adapt tone, style, and content for the particular task at hand." Again, students must "consider the needs of their audiences as they compose, edit, and revise."

Another standard emphasizes that "students apply knowledge of language structure, language conventions. . . ." Students need practice with accepted language conventions (e.g., capitalization, punctuation, grammar) in order to develop awareness and consistent application in their writing.

Language Practice is a program designed for students who require additional practice in the basics of effective writing and speaking. Focused practice in key grammar, usage, mechanics, and composition areas helps students gain ownership of essential skills. The logical sequence of the practice exercises, combined with a clear and concise format, allows for easy and independent use.

National Council of Teachers of English and International Reading Association, *Standards for the English Language Arts*, 1996.

Organization

Language Practice provides systematic, focused attention to just one carefully selected skill at a time. Rules are clearly stated at the beginning of each lesson. Key terms are introduced in bold type. The rules are then illustrated with examples and followed by meaningful practice exercises.

Lessons are organized around a series of units. They are arranged in a logical sequence beginning with vocabulary; progressing through sentences, grammar and usage, and mechanics; and culminating with composition skills.

Grades 3 through 8 include a final unit on study skills, which can be assigned as needed. This unit includes such skills as organizing information, following directions, using a dictionary, using the library, and choosing appropriate reference sources.

Skills are reviewed thoroughly in a two-page test at the conclusion of each unit. These unit tests are presented in a standardized test format. The content of each unit is repeated and expanded in subsequent levels as highlighted in the skills correlation chart on pages 6 and 7.

Use

Throughout the program, *Language Practice* stresses the application of language principles. In addition to matching, circling, or underlining elements in a predetermined sentence, lessons ask students to use what they have learned in an original sentence or in rewriting a sentence.

Language Practice is designed for independent use by students who have had instruction in the specific skills covered in these lessons. Copies of the activities can be given to individuals, pairs of students, or small groups for completion. They can also be used as a center activity. If students are familiar with the content, the worksheets can be homework for reviewing and reinforcing skills.

From the beginning, students feel comfortable with the format of the lessons. Each lesson is introduced with a rule at the top of the page and ends with a meaningful exercise at the bottom of the page. Each lesson is clearly labeled, and directions are clear and uncomplicated. Because the format is logical and consistent and the vocabulary is carefully controlled, most students can use *Language Practice* with a high degree of independence. As the teacher, this allows you the time needed to help students on a one-to-one basis.

Special Feature

The process approach to teaching writing provides success for most students. *Language Practice* provides direct support for the teaching of composition and significantly enhances those strategies and techniques commonly associated with the process-writing approach.

Each book includes a composition unit that provides substantial work with important composition skills, such as considering audience, writing topic sentences, selecting supporting details, taking notes, writing reports, and revising and proofreading. Also included in the composition unit is practice with various prewriting activities, such as clustering and brainstorming, which play an important role in process writing. The composition lessons are presented in the same rule-plus-practice format as in other units.

Additional Notes

- Parent Communication. Sign the *Letter to Parents* and send it home with the students. This letter offers suggestions for parental involvement to increase learner success.

- Assessment Test. Use the Assessment Test on pages 8 through 11 to determine the skills your students need to practice.

- Language Terms. Provide each student with a copy of the list of language terms on page 12 to keep for reference throughout the year. Also place a copy in the classroom language arts center for reference.

- Center Activities. Use the worksheets as center activities to give students the opportunity to work cooperatively.

- Have fun. The activities use a variety of strategies to maintain student interest. Watch your students' language improve as skills are applied in structured, relevant practice!

Dear Parent,

During this school year, our class will be working with a language program that covers the basics of effective writing and speaking. To increase your child's language skills, we will be completing activity sheets that provide practice to ensure mastery of these important skills.

From time to time, I may send home activity sheets. To best help your child, please consider the following suggestions:

- Provide a quiet place to work.
- Go over the rules, examples, and directions together.
- Encourage your child to do his or her best.
- Check the lesson when it is complete.
- Go over your child's work, and note improvements as well as concerns.

Help your child maintain a positive attitude about language skills. Let your child know that each lesson provides an opportunity to have fun and to learn. If your child expresses anxiety about these skills, help him or her understand what causes the stress. Then talk about ways to deal with it in a positive way.

Above all, enjoy this time you spend with your child. He or she will feel your support, and skills will improve with each activity completed.

Thank you for your help!

Cordially,

Skills Correlation

	1	2	3	4	5	6	7	8
Vocabulary								
Sound Words (Onomatopoeia)	■							
Rhyming Words	■	■						
Synonyms	■	■	■	■	■	■	■	■
Antonyms	■	■	■	■	■	■	■	■
Homonyms	■	■	■	■	■	■	■	■
Multiple Meanings/Homographs	■	■	■	■	■	■	■	■
Prefixes and Suffixes			■	■	■	■	■	■
Base and Root Words			■	■	■	■	■	■
Compound Words			■	■	■	■	■	■
Contractions			■	■	■	■	■	■
Idioms						■	■	■
Connotation/Denotation						■	■	■
Sentences								
Word Order in Sentences	■	■						
Recognizing a Sentence	■	■	■	■	■	■	■	■
Subjects and Predicates	■	■	■	■	■	■	■	■
Types of Sentences	■	■	■	■	■	■	■	■
Compound/Complex Sentences			■	■	■	■	■	■
Sentence Combining			■	■	■	■	■	■
Run-On Sentences				■	■	■	■	■
Independent and Subordinate Clauses							■	■
Compound Subjects and Predicates						■	■	■
Direct and Indirect Objects							■	■
Inverted Word Order						■	■	■
Grammar and Usage								
Common and Proper Nouns	■	■	■	■	■	■	■	■
Singular and Plural Nouns	■	■	■	■	■	■	■	■
Possessive Nouns			■	■	■	■	■	■
Appositives						■	■	■
Verbs	■	■	■	■	■	■	■	■
Verb Tense	■	■	■	■	■	■	■	■
Regular/Irregular Verbs	■	■	■	■	■	■	■	■
Subject/Verb Agreement		■	■	■	■	■	■	■
Verb Phrases						■	■	■
Transitive and Intransitive Verbs							■	■
Verbals: Gerunds, Participles, and Infinitives							■	■
Active and Passive Voice							■	■
Mood								■
Pronouns	■	■	■	■	■	■	■	■
Antecedents							■	■
Articles	■	■	■					
Adjectives	■	■	■	■	■	■	■	■
Correct Word Usage (e.g. *may/can, sit/set*)	■	■	■	■	■	■	■	■
Adverbs		■	■	■	■	■	■	■
Prepositions						■	■	■
Prepositional Phrases						■	■	■
Conjunctions						■	■	■
Interjections						■	■	■
Double Negatives								■
Capitalization and Punctuation								
Capitalization: First Word in Sentence	■	■	■	■	■	■	■	
Capitalization: Proper Nouns	■	■	■	■	■	■	■	■
Capitalization: in Letters		■	■	■	■	■	■	■

	1	2	3	4	5	6	7	8
Capitalization and Punctuation (cont'd)								
Capitalization: Abbreviations		■	■	■	■	■	■	■
Capitalization: Titles		■	■	■	■	■	■	■
Capitalization: Proper Adjectives					■	■	■	■
End Punctuation	■	■	■	■	■	■	■	■
Commas		■	■	■	■	■	■	■
Apostrophes in Contractions		■	■	■	■	■	■	■
Apostrophes in Possessives			■	■	■	■	■	■
Quotation Marks			■	■	■	■	■	■
Colons/Semicolons						■	■	■
Hyphens						■	■	■
Composition								
Expanding Sentences					■	■	■	■
Writing a Paragraph		■	■	■	■	■	■	■
Paragraphs: Topic Sentence (main idea)		■	■	■	■	■	■	■
Paragraphs: Supporting Details		■	■	■	■	■	■	■
Order In Paragraphs		■	■	■	■	■	■	
Writing Process:								
Establishing Purpose			■	■		■	■	■
Audience					■	■	■	■
Topic			■	■	■	■	■	■
Outlining				■		■	■	■
Clustering/Brainstorming						■	■	■
Notetaking						■	■	
Revising/Proofreading						■	■	■	■
Types of Writing:								
Letter	■	■	■			■		
"How-to" Paragraph			■					
Invitation			■					
Telephone Message			■					
Conversation				■				
Narrative Paragraph				■				
Comparing and Contrasting					■			
Descriptive Paragraph					■			
Report						■		
Interview							■	
Persuasive Composition								■
Readiness/Study Skills								
Grouping	■							
Letters of Alphabet	■							
Listening	■	■						
Making Comparisons	■	■						
Organizing Information	■	■	■					
Following Directions	■	■	■	■	■			
Alphabetical Order	■	■	■	■	■	■	■	■
Using a Dictionary:								
Definitions		■	■	■	■	■	■	■
Guide Words/Entry Words		■	■	■	■	■	■	■
Syllables			■	■	■	■	■	■
Multiple Meanings						■	■	■
Word Origins						■	■	■
Parts of a Book						■	■	■
Using the Library						■	■	■
Using Encyclopedias				■	■	■	■	■
Using Reference Books						■	■	■
Using the *Readers' Guide*							■	■
Choosing Appropriate Sources						■	■	■

Name _____   Date _____

Assessment Test

A. Write **S** before each pair of synonyms, **A** before each pair of antonyms, and **H** before each pair of homonyms.

_____ **1.** river, stream   _____ **3.** ugly, pretty

_____ **2.** new, knew   _____ **4.** threw, through

B. Write the homograph for the pair of meanings.

_____ **a.** a formal dance   **b.** a round object

C. Write **P** before each word with a prefix, **S** before each word with a suffix, and **C** before each compound word.

_____ **1.** shoelace   _____ **3.** firmness

_____ **2.** mistrust   _____ **4.** downstairs

D. Write the words that make up each contraction.

_____ **1.** won't   _____ **2.** he'll

E. Write **D** before the declarative sentence, **IM** before the imperative sentence, **E** before the exclamatory sentence, and **IN** before the interrogative sentence. Then circle the simple subject, and underline the simple predicate in each sentence.

_____ **1.** Happy days are here again!   _____ **3.** I really like my life right now.

_____ **2.** What do you mean by that?   _____ **4.** You should take it one day at a time.

F. Write **CS** before the sentence with a compound subject. Write **CP** before the sentence with a compound predicate.

_____ **1.** Apples and oranges are my favorite fruits.

_____ **2.** The wind howled and shrieked.

G. Write **CS** before the compound sentence. Write **RO** before the run-on sentence.

_____ **1.** Since it was raining we went inside, we sat and watched it rain.

_____ **2.** It didn't stop raining, so we played card games.

H. Underline the common nouns, and circle the proper nouns in the sentence.

José told Rachel that her dog had been found in the park.

Assessment Test
© Steck-Vaughn Publishing Company

Language Practice 5, SV 7161-9

Name _____   Date _____

I. **Write the correct possessive noun to complete the second sentence.**

The headlight of our car burned out. Our _____ headlight burned out.

J. **Write A if the underlined verb is an action verb, L if it is a linking verb, or H if it is a helping verb.**

_____ **1.** We <u>were</u> waiting our turn.

_____ **2.** It <u>felt</u> good to be there.

_____ **3.** We <u>helped</u> as often as possible.

K. **Write past, present, or future to show the tense of each underlined verb.**

_____ **1.** Someone <u>will come</u> soon.

_____ **2.** They <u>left</u> an hour later.

_____ **3.** She <u>is walking</u> with her children.

L. **Circle the correct verb in each sentence.**

1. (Do, Did) you (see, saw) what happened?

2. He (drink, drank) the water and then (broke, break) the glass.

3. She has (wrote, written) a hit song and has (sang, sung) it on TV.

4. We (eaten, ate) a big meal and (begun, began) to get sleepy.

M. **Write SP before the sentence that has a subject pronoun, OP before the sentence that has an object pronoun, and PP before the sentence that has a possessive pronoun.**

_____ **1.** My grandparents were successful farmers.

_____ **2.** They always lived out in the country.

_____ **3.** Mother told me about the farm.

N. **On the line before each sentence, write adjective or adverb to describe the underlined word.**

_____ **1.** Exercise is part of my <u>daily</u> activities.

_____ **2.** I run <u>often</u>.

O. **In the sentence below, underline each prepositional phrase, and circle each preposition.**

An oil spot was on the floor of the garage.

Name _____ Date _____

P. Circle the correct word in each sentence.

    1. (Teach, Learn) me how to bake.

    2. We will have a (well, good) time together.

    3. Get the eggs, and (sit, set) them on the counter.

    4. Now (sit, set) on the stool.

    5. You (can, may) separate the eggs.

Q. In the letter below, underline letters that should be capitalized, and add punctuation where needed.

                            487 e deer run

                            sacramento ca 94099

                            feb 27 19___

dear luke

  whats it like living in california ___ i cant even imagine it ___ the postcards you sent were fantastic ___ it will be fun to come and visit ___ im worried about earthquakes, though ___

  take care of yourself ___

                            your friend

                            paul

R. Expand the meaning of the sentence base below.

Students created. _____

S. Write a topic sentence and two sentences with descriptive supporting details on the topic of pollution.

_____

_____

_____

T. Number the following directions in order.

_____ **1.** Turn on the dishwasher.

_____ **2.** Load dirty dishes in the machine.

_____ **3.** Put soap in the dispenser.

Assessment Test
© Steck-Vaughn Publishing Company

Language Practice 5, SV 7161-9

U. Read the guide words. Then write the words from the box that would be found on the same page, placing a hyphen between syllables.

slop / sneer

sliding	silver
slumber	smattering
snuggle	sluggish

1. _____

2. _____

3. _____

V. Use the sample encyclopedia entry to answer the questions.

LOCK Locks are sets of gates that help ships move through canals. Each lock is on a different level, and two sets of gates make up each lock. The locks are similar to stairs. A ship moves into a lock, and the gates in front of and behind the ship close. Water is then pumped into or let out of the enclosed lock. This raises or lowers the ship to the level of the next lock. *See also* CANAL.

1. What is the article about? _____

2. What do locks do? _____

3. How many sets of gates does a lock have? _____

4. What are locks compared to in the article? _____

5. What is the cross-reference? _____

W. The example below shows how the volumes of a small encyclopedia are marked. Circle the word you would look under to find an article on each of the following subjects. Then write the number of the volume in which you would find each article.

A–C	D–F	G–H	I–L	M–N	O–R	S–T	U–W	X–Z
1	2	3	4	5	6	7	8	9

_____ **1.** the history of mining

_____ **2.** Mark Twain

_____ **3.** the Nile River

_____ **4.** plant life of the tundra

_____ **5.** the capital of Sweden

_____ **6.** Great Danes

_____ **7.** Japanese gardens

_____ **8.** how volcanoes erupt

Language Terms

abbreviation a short form of a word

action verb a verb that tells an action that the subject is doing

adjective a word that describes a noun by telling which one, what kind, or how many

adverb a word that describes a verb

antonym a word that has the opposite meaning of another word

apostrophe a mark used to show where the missing letter or letters would be in a contraction

common noun a noun that does not name a particular person, place, or thing

compound sentence two simple sentences joined together by words such as and, but, so, and or

compound word a word formed by putting two or more words together

contraction a word formed by joining two other words

declarative sentence a sentence that makes a statement

exclamatory sentence a sentence that shows surprise or emotion

helping verb a word used to help the main verb of the sentence, usually a form of the verb to be

homonym a word that sounds like another word, but has a different meaning and is spelled differently

imperative sentence a sentence that gives a command

interrogative sentence a sentence that asks a question

linking verb a verb that does not show action, but links the subject to a word that either describes the subject or gives the subject another name

noun a word that names a person, place, or thing

object pronoun a pronoun used after an action verb or after words such as to, with, for, and by

paragraph a group of sentences about one main idea

plural noun a noun that names more than one person, place, or thing

possessive noun a noun that tells who or what owns something

possessive pronoun a pronoun that tells who or what owns something

predicate the part of a sentence that tells what the subject does or what happens to the subject

prefix a syllable added to the beginning of a word to change the meaning of the word

pronoun a word that takes the place of a noun

proper noun a noun that names a particular person, place, or thing and is capitalized

quotation tells the exact words a person said

run-on sentence two or more sentences that run together without correct punctuation

sentence a group of words that expresses a complete thought

simple predicate the main word or words in the predicate part of a sentence

simple sentence a sentence that has one subject and one predicate

simple subject the main word in the subject part of a sentence

singular noun a noun that names one person, place, or thing

subject the part of a sentence that tells who or what the sentence is about

suffix a syllable added to the end of a word to change the meaning of the word

synonym a word that has the same or almost the same meaning as another word

topic sentence a sentence that tells the main idea of a paragraph

verb the main word in the predicate

verb tense tells the time expressed by the verb

Synonyms

> ■ A **synonym** is a word that has the same or nearly the same meaning as one or more other words.
> EXAMPLES: help - aid - assist, cold - chilly - wintry

A. Write one synonym for each word below. Write another synonym in a short phrase. Underline the synonym in the phrase.

1. small   little   <u>tiny</u> bug

2. enormous _____ _____

3. vehicle _____ _____

4. select _____ _____

5. complete _____ _____

6. river _____ _____

7. permit _____ _____

8. speedy _____ _____

B. For each word in parentheses, write a synonym in the blank.

1. Many trees in an old forest are (high) _____ .

2. Underneath them grow (lower) _____ trees and plants.

3. As the (aged) _____ trees die, they make room for others.

4. Sometimes fires will (destroy) _____ the entire forest.

5. Then from the (charred) _____ earth sprout new plants.

6. They all begin their (stretch) _____ for the sky again.

C. Write three sentences about the forest. In each sentence, use a synonym for one of the words below. Underline the synonym.

begin	lofty	soil

1. _____

2. _____

3. _____

Antonyms

> ■ An **antonym** is a word that has the opposite meaning of another word. EXAMPLES: hot - cold, tall - short

A. Write an antonym for the underlined word in each phrase below.

1. <u>dark</u> blue _____
2. <u>busy</u> worker _____
3. <u>up</u> the hill _____
4. <u>noisy</u> play _____
5. <u>north</u> wind _____
6. <u>buy</u> a car _____
7. time of <u>day</u> _____
8. <u>bitter</u> taste _____
9. <u>come</u> now _____
10. <u>good</u> dog _____
11. <u>small</u> bird _____
12. <u>rough</u> road _____
13. <u>black</u> coat _____
14. <u>above</u> the neck _____

15. <u>frowning</u> face _____
16. <u>under</u> the bridge _____
17. <u>pretty</u> color _____
18. <u>cold</u> water _____
19. feeling <u>strong</u> _____
20. <u>wide</u> belt _____
21. <u>unhappy</u> face _____
22. <u>east</u> side _____
23. <u>cool</u> breeze _____
24. <u>stop</u> the car _____
25. <u>heavy</u> jacket _____
26. <u>long</u> story _____
27. <u>give</u> a gift _____
28. <u>difficult</u> task _____

B. For each word in parentheses, write an antonym in the blank.

We were very (sad) _____ to be on vacation. It

was the (last) _____ time we had been able to (stay)

_____ in a long time, and this one would be really (boring)

_____ . We rented a cabin in the (low) _____

mountains of Colorado. We were hoping for (hot) _____

and snowy weather so we could ski. The (last) _____ thing

we did when we got to the cabin was (pack) _____ our

clothes. Then we hiked around (inside) _____ . We liked

being in such a (terrible) _____ place.

Homonyms

> ■ **Homonyms** are words that are pronounced alike but are spelled differently and have different meanings.
>   EXAMPLES: I'll – aisle   two – too – to

A. **Write a short phrase that includes a homonym for each word below. Circle each homonym.**

1. haul ____long (hall)____   4. way _____

2. road _____   5. new _____

3. sum _____   6. meat _____

> ■ **Two** is a number. **Too** means "also," "besides," or "more than enough." **To** means "toward." It is also used with such words as be, sing, play, and other action words.

B. **Fill in the blanks with two, too, or to.**

1. Ben was _____ frightened _____ utter a word.

2. He had heard the strange sound _____ times.

3. He went _____ his room upstairs, _____ steps at a time.

   But he heard it there, _____.

4. He decided _____ call his friend who lived _____ blocks away.

   It seemed the only thing _____ do!

> ■ **Their** means "belonging to them." **There** means "in that place." **They're** is a contraction of the words they are.

C. **Underline the correct word in parentheses.**

1. They are over (their, there, they're) standing in (their, there, they're) yard.

2. (Their, There, They're) waiting to go visit (their, there, they're) friends.

3. (Their, There, They're) going to leave for (their, there, they're) vacation.

Homographs

> ■ **Homographs** are words that are spelled the same but have different meanings. They may also be pronounced differently.
> EXAMPLE: desert meaning "a barren, dry place" and desert also meaning "to abandon"

A. Read each sentence and the two meanings for the underlined word. Circle the meaning that tells how the word is used in the sentence.

1. The soldiers' arms were old and rusty.

   a. parts of the body   b. weapons for war

2. Several had made bats from fallen tree limbs.

   a. flying mammals   b. rounded wooden clubs

3. The long war had made them all tired.

   a. extending over a considerable time   b. to wish for

4. They were all ready to go back home.

   a. part of the body   b. to a place from which a person came

5. They hoped someone would lead them to safety.

   a. soft, gray metal   b. to show the way

B. Write the homograph for each pair of meanings below. The first letter of each word is given for you.

1. a. sound made with fingers   b. a metal fastener   s_____

2. a. lame walk or step   b. not stiff   l_____

3. a. use oars to move a boat   b. a noisy fight   r_____

4. a. a tree covering   b. the sound a dog makes   b_____

5. a. to press flat   b. a yellow vegetable   s_____

C. Write pairs of sentences that show two different meanings for each homograph below. Use a dictionary if necessary.

1. school _____

   _____

2. pupil _____

   _____

Prefixes and Suffixes

> - A **prefix** or a **suffix** added to a base word changes the meaning of the word.
>   EXAMPLE: re- meaning "again" + the base word <u>do</u> = <u>redo</u> meaning "to do again"
> - Re- means "again," pre- means "before," <u>mis</u>- means "wrongly" or "not," <u>-able</u> means "that can be," <u>-less</u> means "without," <u>-ness</u> means "state of being."

A. Write the word formed by each combination. Then write the definition of the new word.

1. kind + ness = _____

2. pre + date = _____

3. help + less = _____

4. re + made = _____

B. Read each sentence. Use one of the prefixes or suffixes and the base word below each blank to form a new word. Write the new word in the blank.

mis- -ful pre- -less re- -ness

1. Terry _____ her vacation by viewing the photographs
     (lives)
she took.

2. She spends _____ hours enjoying the mountain scenery.
                 (end)

3. Her favorite shot shows a mountain sunset just before

_____ settled over their campsite.
     (dark)

4. John didn't see Terry's look of fright when a bear made

a _____ raid on the garbage can.
     (dawn)

5. John had _____ the camera directions in the dim light.
              (read)

6. He did, however, get a shot of the bear's _____ cubs.
                                              (delight)

Contractions

> ■ A **contraction** is a word formed by joining two other words. An apostrophe shows where a letter or letters have been left out.   EXAMPLES: it is = it's   we will = we'll

A. Write the contraction formed by the words.

1. who + is = _____

2. could + not = _____

3. they + have = _____

4. I + will = _____

5. does + not = _____

6. should + have = _____

7. you + would = _____

8. I + have = _____

9. that + is = _____

10. did + not = _____

11. let + us = _____

12. they + are = _____

B. Use the contractions below to complete each sentence. Write the contractions on the lines.

can't	couldn't	he'll	I'm	it's	I've	Let's
She's	wasn't	What'll	What's	Where's		

1. It _____ quite show time.

2. José called out, "_____ Pearl?"

3. "What?" shouted Sara. "_____ not here yet?"

4. "No, and _____ looked everywhere."

5. "The show _____ go on without the star," Sara wailed.

6. Sara added, "_____ we do?"

7. "_____ ask Adam," José suggested.

8. "Yes," said Sara, "_____ know what to do."

9. Just then a voice called, "_____ all the excitement?"

10. "Pearl, _____ you!" Sara and José exclaimed.

11. "Yes," said Pearl, "I know _____ late."

12. Pearl added, "I _____ find my costume!"

Compound Words

> ■ **Compound words** may be two words written as one, two
> words joined by a hyphen, or two separate words.
> EXAMPLES: sunlight   ho-hum   easy chair

A. Draw a line between the two words that form each compound word below.

1. highway	6. fire drill	11. highrise
2. old-time	7. barefoot	12. earthquake
3. full moon	8. baby-sitter	13. half-mast
4. snowflake	9. splashdown	14. bulldog
5. air conditioner	10. sweatshirt	15. skateboard

B. Use two of the words below to form a compound word that will complete each numbered sentence. Write the word on the blank.

after	back	come	hard	hood	neighbor	noon	out	ware	yard

1. Jan and I bought a hammer and nails at a _____ store.

2. Part of the fence in our _____ was broken.

3. It took most of the _____ to repair the fence.

4. We were proud of the _____.

5. Our fence was the finest in the _____.

C. Use the second word part of each compound word to make the next compound word. Write the new word.

1. clubhouse   a building used by a club

   _____houseboat_____   a boat that people can live in

   _____boathouse_____   a house for storing boats

2. teacup   a cup for drinking tea

   _____   a cake the size of a cup

   _____   a circular walking game in which players may win
                               a cake

Unit 1 Test

Choose whether the underlined words in each sentence are synonyms, antonyms, homonyms, or homographs.

1. My <u>aunt</u> gave me an <u>ant</u> farm for my birthday.
   A ○ synonyms **B** ○ antonyms **C** ○ homonyms **D** ○ homographs

2. The tree <u>grew</u> taller and <u>increased</u> in size.
   A ○ synonyms **B** ○ antonyms **C** ○ homonyms **D** ○ homographs

3. Susan seemed <u>happy</u>, but inside she was <u>unhappy</u>.
   A ○ synonyms **B** ○ antonyms **C** ○ homonyms **D** ○ homographs

4. Did the <u>knight</u> travel by day or by <u>night</u>?
   A ○ synonyms **B** ○ antonyms **C** ○ homonyms **D** ○ homographs

5. John <u>left</u> the room and turned <u>left</u> down the hall.
   A ○ synonyms **B** ○ antonyms **C** ○ homonyms **D** ○ homographs

6. I traded the <u>dull</u> movie for an <u>exciting</u> book.
   A ○ synonyms **B** ○ antonyms **C** ○ homonyms **D** ○ homographs

7. She soon <u>saw</u> that the blade of the <u>saw</u> was bent.
   A ○ synonyms **B** ○ antonyms **C** ○ homonyms **D** ○ homographs

8. He heard her <u>shout</u>, and then gave a <u>yell</u> to call for help.
   A ○ synonyms **B** ○ antonyms **C** ○ homonyms **D** ○ homographs

Add a prefix or suffix to the underlined word to make a new word that makes sense in the sentence.

9. Beth was able to <u>pay</u> John the money she borrowed.
   A ○ mis-   **C** ○ -ity
   B ○ re-   **D** ○ -less

10. We had a <u>delight</u> vacation.
    A ○ -er   **C** ○ -ful
    B ○ pre-   **D** ○ -ment

11. I like to spend <u>end</u> hours reading.
    A ○ -er   **C** ○ -less
    B ○ -ity   **D** ○ un-

12. How did Janet <u>act</u> to the news?
    A ○ -er   **C** ○ pro-
    B ○ re-   **D** ○ -ment

13. <u>Dark</u> settled over the campsite.
    A ○ -er   **C** ○ -al
    B ○ bi-   **D** ○ -ness

14. We can't <u>read</u> the directions!
    A ○ bi-   **C** ○ mis-
    B ○ pro-   **D** ○ -less

Choose the correct contraction for each pair of underlined words.

15. it is
    A ○ its   C ○ i'ts
    B ○ its'   D ○ it's

16. we had
    A ○ w'd   C ○ we'ad
    B ○ w'ed   D ○ we'd

17. they are
    A ○ the'yre   C ○ they're
    B ○ the'are   D ○ theyr'e

18. who would
    A ○ who'd   C ○ who'uld
    B ○ who'wd   D ○ who'ud

19. do not
    A ○ don'ot   C ○ do'not
    B ○ dont'   D ○ don't

20. she will
    A ○ shel'l   C ○ she'll
    B ○ shell'   D ○ sh'ell

Choose the two words that make up each underlined contraction.

21. I'll
    A ○ I would   C ○ I have
    B ○ I did   D ○ I will

22. they've
    A ○ they have C ○ they would
    B ○ they will D ○ they are

23. he'd
    A ○ he did   C ○ he would
    B ○ he could   D ○ he said

24. we're
    A ○ we were   C ○ we have
    B ○ we are   D ○ we will

Choose the word that combines with the word in parentheses to make a compound word that completes the sentence.

25. The Dorn family lives on a (house) _____ .
    A ○ shoe   C ○ top
    B ○ boat   D ○ branch

26. The bird was perched in the (tree) _____ .
    A ○ trunk   C ○ top
    B ○ root   D ○ branch

27. I knew it was (some) _____ serious.
    A ○ matter   C ○ day
    B ○ thing   D ○ time

28. He held his breath (under) _____ .
    A ○ way   C ○ ground
    B ○ side   D ○ water

29. I love (summer) _____ .
    A ○ time   C ○ vacation
    B ○ sun   D ○ best

30. The handle on my (suit) _____ broke.
    A ○ coat   C ○ swim
    B ○ case   D ○ hanger

Recognizing Sentences

■ A **sentence** is a group of words that expresses a complete thought.   EXAMPLE: Many readers like stories about dogs.

A. Some of the groups of words below are sentences, and some are not. Write S before each group that is a sentence.

_____ 1. One famous dog story.

_____ 2. First appeared in a well-known magazine.

_____ 3. You may have read this famous story.

_____ 4. A collie named Lassie, who was owned by a poor farmer in Yorkshire, England.

_____ 5. To make money for his family.

_____ 6. The farmer sold Lassie to a wealthy duke.

_____ 7. Lassie was loyal to her first master, however.

_____ 8. Taken hundreds of miles from Yorkshire.

_____ 9. She found her way back to her first home.

_____ 10. The story became a book and then a movie.

_____ 11. Helped two child actors on their way to stardom.

_____ 12. The real-life Lassie was a dog named Toots.

_____ 13. Toots was the companion of Eric Knight, the author of the story.

_____ 14. Lived in Yorkshire as a boy, but in the United States as an adult.

_____ 15. Knight died before his story, "Lassie Come Home," became famous.

_____ 16. Was killed in World War II.

_____ 17. Toots died on Knight's farm two years later.

B. Write a sentence about one of your favorite books.

_____

Name _____   Date _____

Types of Sentences

> ■ A **declarative** sentence makes a statement.
>   EXAMPLE: The telephone is ringing.
> ■ An **interrogative** sentence asks a question.
>   EXAMPLE: Where are you going?

A. Write <u>declarative</u> or <u>interrogative</u> after each sentence in the conversation below.

1. When did you get those new rollerblades? _____

2. I bought them yesterday. _____

3. Don't you think rollerblading is dangerous? _____

4. It's not any more dangerous than skateboarding. _____

5. I would like to learn to rollerblade. _____

6. Will you teach me? _____

7. Do you have a pair of rollerblades? _____

8. No, but I will buy some tomorrow. _____

B. Pretend that you are talking to the inventor of a new way to travel over land, sea, or in the air. Write four questions you'd ask and the inventor's answers. Label each sentence <u>D</u> for declarative or <u>I</u> for interrogative.

1. _____ _____

2. _____ _____

3. _____ _____

4. _____ _____

5. _____ _____

6. _____ _____

7. _____ _____

8. _____ _____

Name _____   Date _____

More Types of Sentences

> ■ An **imperative** sentence expresses a command or a request.
>   EXAMPLES: Answer the telephone. Please don't shout.
> ■ An **exclamatory** sentence expresses strong or sudden feeling.
>   EXAMPLES: What a great movie! They're off!

A. Write <u>imperative</u> or <u>exclamatory</u> after each sentence.

1. Listen to that strange noise. _____

2. What a weird sound that is! _____

3. Go see what's there. _____

4. Go yourself. _____

5. I'm too scared! _____

6. Then look out the window. _____

7. What a cute kitten that is! _____

8. We shouldn't be scared! _____

9. Go get the kitten. _____

10. Come with me. _____

11. Oh, look! _____

12. Count the rest of the kittens in the basket. _____

13. Read the note attached to the handle. _____

14. What a surprise! _____

B. Write about a time you or someone you know was frightened by something. Use at least one exclamatory sentence and one imperative sentence.

_____

_____

_____

_____

Complete Subjects and Predicates

> - Every sentence has two main parts — a **complete subject** and a **complete predicate.**
> - The complete subject includes all the words that name the person, place, or thing about which something is said.
>   EXAMPLE: **My sister Sara** plays tennis.
> - The complete predicate includes all the words that tell what the subject is or does.
>   EXAMPLE: My sister Sara **plays tennis.**

A. Write <u>S</u> before each group of words that may be used as a complete subject. Write <u>P</u> before each group of words that may be used as a complete predicate.

_____ **1.** the mayor of our town

_____ **2.** has a large town square

_____ **3.** celebrate the holidays with parades

_____ **4.** an election every four years

_____ **5.** a map with every street in town

_____ **6.** were planning to build a new swimming pool

B. Complete each sentence by writing a subject or a predicate.

1. All our town council members _____.

2. _____ met in an important meeting.

3. _____ explained the problem.

4. Every interested citizen _____.

5. Our town's first settlers _____.

6. _____ planted crops.

7. _____ has been abandoned for years.

8. _____ should be preserved.

9. Some people _____.

10. _____ will have to come to vote.

11. My entire family _____.

Simple Subjects

> - The **simple subject** of a sentence is the main word in the complete subject.   EXAMPLE: My friends <u>go mushroom hunting</u>. The words <u>My friends</u> make up the complete subject. The word <u>friends</u> is the simple subject.
> - If the subject is made up of just one word, that word is both the complete subject and the simple subject.
>   EXAMPLE: **I** go mushroom hunting with my friends.

A. In each sentence below, draw a line between the subject and the predicate. Underline the complete subject. Circle the simple subject.

1. Freshly-picked (morels) are delicious.

2. These mushrooms can be found only in the spring.

3. A rich soil is best for morels.

4. Grassy spots are good places to look.

5. The spring must not be dry or too cold.

6. Damp earth is a good sign that morels may be found.

7. A clear, sunny sky means good hunting.

8. We never know where we'll find morels.

9. Tall, wet grasses often hide them.

10. We must work fast.

11. These spongy little mushrooms do not last long.

12. You might like to join us sometime.

B. Write five sentences about an activity you enjoy. Draw a line between the subject and the predicate. Underline the complete subject. Circle the simple subject.

1. _____

2. _____

3. _____

4. _____

5. _____

Simple Predicates

> - The **simple predicate** of a sentence is a verb within the complete predicate. The verb is an action or being word.
>   EXAMPLE: The Netherlands attracts many tourists. The words attracts many tourists make up the complete predicate. The verb attracts is the simple predicate.
> - The simple predicate may be a one-word verb or a verb of more than one word.
>   EXAMPLES: Joan **likes** tulips. She **is planning** a garden.

A. **In each sentence below, draw a line between the subject and the predicate. Underline the complete predicate twice. Circle the simple predicate.**

1. Many tourists visit the Netherlands in April or May.
2. The beautiful tulip blooms reach their height of glory during these months.
3. Visitors can see flowers for miles and miles.
4. Joan is dreaming of a trip to the Netherlands someday.
5. She has seen colorful pictures of tulips in catalogs.
6. The catalogs show tulips of all colors in full bloom.
7. Joan is anxious to see the tulips herself.
8. Passing travelers can buy large bunches of flowers.
9. Every Dutch city has flowers everywhere.
10. Flower vases can be found in the cars of some Dutch people.

B. **Add a predicate for each subject below. Circle the simple predicate.**

1. My neighbor's garden _____.

2. I _____.

3. All of the flowers _____.

C. **Write four sentences about a city or a country that you would like to visit or have visited. Draw a line between the subject and the predicate. Underline the complete predicate twice. Circle the simple predicate.**

1. _____
2. _____
3. _____
4. _____

Understood Subjects

> ■ The subject of an imperative sentence is always the person to whom the command or request is given **(You).** The subject does not appear in the sentence. Therefore, it is called an **understood subject.**   EXAMPLES: **(You)** Keep off the grass.   **(You)** Close the door, please.

A. **On the line after each imperative sentence below, write the understood subject and the simple predicate.**

1. Turn left at the next light.   _____(You) Turn_____

2. Now turn right on Elm Street.   _____

3. Park in front of the house.   _____

4. Don't block the driveway.   _____

5. Leave enough room for them to leave.   _____

6. Help me with the food, please.   _____

7. Hold the door open until I get out.   _____

8. Get the bag off the back seat.   _____

9. Lock the car door, please.   _____

10. Check to see that the lights are off.   _____

11. Knock harder on the door.   _____

12. Try ringing the doorbell.   _____

B. **Write four imperative sentences about a game or other activity. After each sentence, write the understood subject.**

1. _____

2. _____

3. _____

4. _____

Using Compound Subjects

> ■ Two sentences that have different subjects but the same predicate can be combined to make one sentence. The two subjects are joined by <u>and</u>. The subject of the new sentence is called a **compound subject.**   EXAMPLE: **Craig** likes tall tales. **Jack** likes tall tales. **Craig and Jack** like tall tales.

A. In each sentence below, underline the subject. If the subject is compound, write C before the sentence.

_____ 1. Paul Bunyan and Babe were the subject of many tall tales.

_____ 2. Babe was Paul's blue ox.

_____ 3. Maine and Minnesota are two of the states that have tall tales about Paul and Babe.

_____ 4. Babe could haul the timber from 640 acres at one time.

_____ 5. Lumberjacks and storytellers liked to tell tall tales about Paul and Babe's great deeds.

B. Combine each pair of sentences below to make a sentence that has a compound subject. Underline the compound subject.

1. Tennessee claims Davy Crockett as its hero. Texas claims Davy Crockett as its hero.

_____

2. Great bravery made Davy Crockett famous. Unusual skills made Davy Crockett famous.

_____

3. True stories about Davy Crockett were passed down. Tall tales about Davy Crockett were passed down.

_____

4. These true stories made Davy Crockett a legend. These tall tales made Davy Crockett a legend.

_____

C. Write a sentence using Paul Bunyan and Davy Crockett as the subject.

_____

_____

Using Compound Predicates

> ■ Two sentences that have the same subject but different predicates can be combined to make one sentence. The two predicates may be joined by <u>or</u>, <u>and</u>, or <u>but</u>. The predicate of the sentence is called a **compound predicate.**
>
> EXAMPLE: A newspaper **informs its readers.** A newspaper **entertains its readers.** A newspaper **informs and entertains its readers.**

A. In each sentence below, underline the predicate. If the predicate is compound, write <u>C</u> before the sentence.

_____ 1. Our class wrote and printed its own newspaper.

_____ 2. Leslie was named editor-in-chief.

_____ 3. She assigned the stories and approved the final copies.

_____ 4. Wong and several other students were reporters.

_____ 5. They either wrote the news stories or edited the stories.

_____ 6. Wong interviewed a new student and wrote up the interview.

B. Combine each pair of sentences below to make a sentence that has a compound predicate. Underline the compound predicate.

1. Jenny covered the baseball game. Jenny described the best plays.

_____

2. Sue and Kim wrote jokes. Sue and Kim made up puzzles.

_____

3. Luis corrected the news stories. Luis wrote headlines.

_____

4. Alex typed the newspaper. Alex couldn't print the newspaper.

_____

C. Imagine that you are Luis or Jenny. Write a sentence that has a compound predicate which could begin the story on the baseball game.

_____

_____

Simple and Compound Sentences

- A **simple sentence** has one subject and one predicate.
  EXAMPLE: The United States' presidents/led interesting lives.
- A **compound sentence** is made up of two simple sentences
  joined by connecting words such as <u>and</u>, <u>but</u>, and <u>or</u>. A comma
  is placed before the connecting word.
  EXAMPLE: George Washington led the army in the
  Revolutionary War, **and** Ulysses S. Grant led it in the Civil War.

**A. Draw a line between each subject and predicate. Write <u>S</u> before each
simple sentence. Write <u>C</u> before each compound sentence.**

_____ 1. George Washington witnessed the first successful balloon flight.

_____ 2. John Adams was our second president, and his son was our sixth.

_____ 3. Thomas Jefferson was very interested in experiments with balloons
and submarines.

_____ 4. The British burned the White House in 1814, but President
Madison escaped unharmed.

B. Combine each pair of simple sentences below into a compound sentence.

1. Andrew Jackson was called "Old Hickory."
   Zachary Taylor's nickname was "Old Rough and Ready."

   _____

   _____

2. Four presidents had no children. John Tyler had fourteen children.

   _____

   _____

3. Chester A. Arthur put the first bathroom in the White
   House. Benjamin Harrison put in electric lights.

   _____

   _____

4. Woodrow Wilson coached college football. Ronald Reagan
   announced baseball games on radio.

   _____

   _____

Name _____   Date _____

Correcting Run-on Sentences

- Two or more sentences that are run together without the correct punctuation are called a **run-on sentence**.
  EXAMPLE: Animals that carry their young in the mother's pouch are called marsupials, they live mainly in Australia.
- Correct a run-on sentence by making separate sentences from its parts.
  EXAMPLE: Animals that carry their young in the mother's pouch are called marsupials. They live mainly in Australia.

A. Separate the run-on sentences below. Write the last word of the first sentence. Place a period after the word. Then write the first word of the second sentence. Be sure to capitalize the word. One run-on sentence is made of three sentences.

1. There are over two hundred kinds of marsupials all live in North or South America or in Australia.

   1. _____ marsupials.
      _____ All

2. The kangaroo is the largest marsupial, the male red kangaroo may be up to seven feet tall.

   2. _____
      _____

3. Wallabies are similar to kangaroos, they are smaller than kangaroos, some are the size of a rabbit.

   3. _____
      _____
      _____
      _____

4. Kangaroos and wallabies live only in Australia, their hind feet are larger than their front feet.

   4. _____
      _____

B. Correct the run-on sentences in the paragraph below. Use the proofreader's symbols as shown in parentheses. (The opossum is active at night⁄ it plays dead if frightened.) There will be seven sentences.

Opossums are the only marsupials that live north of Mexico, they also live in Central and South America. Opossums are grayish white, they have a long snout, hairless ears, and a long, hairless tail. Opossums have fifty teeth, the opossum mother has from five to twenty babies, each baby is the size of a kidney bean.

Unit 2 Test

Choose the group of words that is a sentence.

1. A ○ A huge map of the town.
   B ○ I located the school on the map.
   C ○ Couldn't find my house.
   D ○ Where is?

2. A ○ So could meet.
   B ○ Before we leave.
   C ○ Saw us last week!
   D ○ Jim plays the piano.

Choose whether each sentence is declarative, interrogative, imperative, or exclamatory.

3. How did Tom injure his thumb?
   A ○ declarative
   B ○ interrogative
   C ○ imperative
   D ○ exclamatory

5. Get a bandage for Tom.
   A ○ declarative
   B ○ interrogative
   C ○ imperative
   D ○ exclamatory

4. He cut it on a tin can.
   A ○ declarative
   B ○ interrogative
   C ○ imperative
   D ○ exclamatory

6. What a bad cut it was!
   A ○ declarative
   B ○ interrogative
   C ○ imperative
   D ○ exclamatory

Choose which part of each sentence is underlined.

7. The seasons are four parts of a year.
   A ○ simple subject
   B ○ simple predicate
   C ○ complete subject
   D ○ complete predicate

9. Winter makes some people sad.
   A ○ simple subject
   B ○ simple predicate
   C ○ complete subject
   D ○ complete predicate

8. Spring and summer are warm.
   A ○ simple subject
   B ○ simple predicate
   C ○ complete subject
   D ○ complete predicate

10. Other people feel just the opposite.
   A ○ simple subject
   B ○ simple predicate
   C ○ complete subject
   D ○ complete predicate

Choose the correct answer to each question.

11. In which sentence is the simple subject underlined?

A ○ My <u>friend</u> has a neat workshop.

B ○ He has <u>all kinds</u> of tools.

C ○ <u>My favorite tool</u> is the jigsaw.

D ○ Joe and I <u>cut</u> pieces for puzzles.

12. In which sentence is the complete predicate underlined?

A ○ <u>Kim</u> joined the band.

B ○ She <u>can</u> play the drums.

C ○ Our band marched <u>in a parade</u>.

D ○ My little brother <u>waved to me</u>.

13. In which sentence is the compound predicate underlined?

A ○ All living things <u>grow and die</u>.

B ○ Animals and plants <u>breathe differently</u>.

C ○ Some <u>plants and animals</u> can live underwater.

D ○ Others <u>must</u> live on land.

14. In which sentence is the compound subject underlined?

A ○ Ted finished <u>wrapping</u> the package.

B ○ <u>Ribbons and bows</u> made it colorful.

C ○ He used <u>glue</u> and tape.

D ○ It was very <u>hard for Erin</u> to open.

Choose the sentence that is the best combination of the two simple sentences.

15. The planet Mercury doesn't have any moons. Venus doesn't have any moons.

A ○ Mercury is a planet, and so is Venus.

B ○ Mercury has no moons, neither does Venus.

C ○ Mercury and Venus do not have any moons.

D ○ Mercury and Venus have moons, but we can't see them.

16. Venus is similar to Earth. Venus is hotter than Earth.

A ○ Venus is different from Earth.

B ○ Earth is colder than Venus.

C ○ Venus is similar to Earth, but it is hotter.

D ○ Venus and Earth are the same size.

Choose the answer that correctly describes each sentence.

17. The driver pulled over, and then he stopped.

A ○ simple

B ○ compound

C ○ run-on

D ○ not a sentence

18. He avoided an accident.

A ○ simple

B ○ compound

C ○ run-on

D ○ not a sentence

Nouns

> ■ A **noun** is a word that names a person, place, thing, or quality.   EXAMPLES: Rachel, Chad, city, Montana, shell, animal, love, freedom, happiness

A. Write nouns that name the following:

1. Four people you admire

   _____   _____

   _____   _____

2. Four places you would like to visit

   _____   _____

   _____   _____

3. Six things you use every day

   _____   _____

   _____   _____

   _____   _____

4. Four qualities you would like to have

   _____   _____

   _____   _____

5. Four states in the United States

   _____   _____

   _____   _____

B. Find and underline twenty-six nouns in the sentences below.

1. Every section of the United States has scenes of natural beauty.
2. The tall trees in California are called the giants of the forest.
3. Every fall, tourists go to see the colorful trees in Vermont.
4. Southern coastal cities are proud of their sandy beaches.
5. Colorful flowers and grasses cover the prairies of Texas.
6. Montana and Wyoming boast of majestic mountains.
7. The citizens of every state take pride in the charm of their own state.

Common and Proper Nouns

- There are two main classes of nouns: **common** and **proper nouns.**
- A **common noun** is a word that names any one of a class of objects.   EXAMPLES: girl, city, dog
- A **proper noun** is the name of a particular person, place, or thing. It begins with a capital letter.
    EXAMPLES: Sue, Nashville, Digger

A. Write a proper noun for each common noun below.

1. city _____   10. street _____

2. school _____   11. game _____

3. friend _____   12. river _____

4. ocean _____   13. woman _____

5. state _____   14. country _____

6. car _____   15. man _____

7. singer _____   16. president _____

8. day _____   17. month _____

9. lake _____   18. planet _____

B. Write a common noun for each proper noun below.

1. Alaska _____   10. South America _____

2. November _____   11. Dr. Cooke _____

3. Thanksgiving _____   12. Rocky Mountains _____

4. Beth _____   13. Abraham Lincoln _____

5. December _____   14. Sahara _____

6. Hawaii _____   15. Denver _____

7. *Call of the Wild* _____   16. Mexico _____

8. Saturday _____   17. Saturn _____

9. Manitoba _____   18. Jason _____

Name _____ Date _____

Singular and Plural Nouns

> ■ A **singular noun** is a noun that names one person, place, or thing.   EXAMPLES: knife, church, boy, mouse
> ■ A **plural noun** is a noun that names more than one person, place, or thing.   EXAMPLES: knives, churches, boys, mice

A. Write **S** before each singular noun below. Then write its plural form. Write **P** before each plural noun. Then write its singular form. You may wish to check the spellings in a dictionary.

_____ 1. boots _____   _____ 9. baby _____

_____ 2. army _____   _____ 10. women _____

_____ 3. match _____   _____ 11. halves _____

_____ 4. maps _____   _____ 12. skies _____

_____ 5. inches _____   _____ 13. wife _____

_____ 6. foot _____   _____ 14. boxes _____

_____ 7. hero _____   _____ 15. beach _____

_____ 8. alley _____   _____ 16. book _____

B. Write the plural form of each word below to complete the sentences.

watch	shelf	child	story	monkey	player

1. There are many interesting _____ in that magazine.

2. The cover story on timepieces describes the making of _____ .

3. A sports story contains conversations with three of the nation's leading

   football _____ .

4. A do-it-yourself article shows how to build _____ that will hold an aquarium.

5. Unusual _____ and apes are shown in a picture story.

6. This month's special article is a selection of poems and stories by

   German _____ .

Name _____   Date _____

Singular Possessive Nouns

> - A **possessive noun** shows possession of the noun that follows.   EXAMPLES: mother's car, the dog's bone
> - To form the possessive of most singular nouns, add an apostrophe (') and -s.   EXAMPLES: Sally's room, the city's mayor

A. **Write the possessive form of the noun in parentheses to complete each phrase.**

1. the _____ leash   (dog)

2. the _____ lawn   (neighbor)

3. one of the _____ engines   (plane)

4. _____ greatest ambition   (Ann)

5. to _____ house   (grandmother)

6. the _____ paw   (tiger)

7. my _____ farm   (sister)

8. your _____ best friend   (brother)

9. our _____ advice   (mother)

10. the _____ gym   (school)

11. my _____ apple   (teacher)

12. that _____ fur   (cat)

13. the _____ teeth   (dinosaur)

14. the _____ coach   (team)

B. **Write each of the phrases below in a shorter way.**

1. the friend of Amanda   _____Amanda's friend_____

2. the car of the friend   _____

3. the keeper of the zoo   _____

4. the roar of the lion   _____

5. the cage of the tiger   _____

Plural Possessive Nouns

- To form the possessive of a plural noun ending in -s, add only an apostrophe.
  EXAMPLES: the boys' coats, the books' covers
- To form the possessive of a plural noun that does not end in -s, add an apostrophe and -s.
  EXAMPLES: men's suits, children's toys

A. Complete the chart below. You may wish to check the spellings in a dictionary.

Singular noun	Plural noun	Singular possessive	Plural possessive
1. horse	horses	horse's	horses'
2. bird			
3. teacher			
4. child			
5. truck			
6. doctor			
7. man			
8. church			

B. Rewrite each sentence using a possessive noun.

1. The cat of the Smiths has three kittens.

   _____

2. The names of the kittens are Frisky, Midnight, and Puff.

   _____

3. The dogs of the neighbors are very playful.

   _____

4. The pen of the dogs is in the yard.

   _____

5. The curiosity of the cats might get them into trouble.

   _____

Name _____   Date _____

Action Verbs

- A **verb** is a word that shows action. The verb may show action that can be seen.
  EXAMPLE: Jane **opened** the door.
- The verb may show action that cannot be seen.
  EXAMPLE: Mary **thought** about it.

A. Underline the verb in each sentence.

1. Several years ago people <u>started</u> recycling materials.
2. Today people recycle many things.
3. They buy special containers to sort their wastes.
4. In years past, few people recycled.
5. People threw most of their trash away.
6. Some people burned their trash.
7. This harmed the environment.
8. Then groups of people asked companies to recycle used materials.
9. Today many companies recycle materials.
10. People throw less trash away.
11. Many groups work hard to encourage recycling.
12. Responsible companies now recycle many things.

B. Complete each sentence with one of the verbs below.
Use each verb once.

believe	felt	hoped	knew	remember	studied	thought	worried

1. Yoko really _____ about the math test.

2. She _____ every day.

3. She _____ she could pass the test.

4. During the test, Yoko _____ carefully about each problem.

5. Could she _____ all she had studied?

6. She _____ more confident once the test was over.

7. She _____ that she had done well.

8. When Yoko got her test back, she couldn't _____ she got an A!

Helping Verbs

> - A verb may have a **main verb** and one or more **helping verbs.**
>   Such a verb is called a **verb phrase.**
>   EXAMPLES: The bells **were ringing.** Where **have** you
>   **been hiding?**

A. Underline each main verb. Circle each helping verb. Some verbs do not have a helping verb.

1. (Have) you <u>heard</u> of Casey Jones?

2. He was born John Luther Jones in Cayce (Kay' see), Kentucky.

3. As a railroad engineer, he could make sad music with

    his locomotive whistle.

4. Soon people were telling stories about Casey.

5. One of the stories was about his train wreck.

6. One day he had climbed into his engine cab.

7. The train was carrying the mail.

8. It had been pouring rain for more than a week.

9. The railroad track was covered with water.

10. They were running late.

11. But maybe they could make it on time!

12. Around a curve, they saw a passenger train.

13. Everyone jumped.

14. But Casey did his job, faithful and true to the end.

15. People still sing about this brave railroad man.

B. Complete each sentence by adding <u>have</u>, <u>will</u>, or <u>would</u>.

1. Marla and Ricardo _____ like to go swimming.

2. They _____ received permission from their parents.

3. This _____ be their second trip to the pool today.

Name _____   Date _____

Present and Past Tense

> - A verb in the **present tense** shows an action that happens now.   EXAMPLE: I **watch** TV.
> - A verb in the **past tense** shows an action that happened in the past.   EXAMPLE: I **watched** TV.

A. Underline each verb in the present tense.

1. A famous poem tells about another Casey.
2. This Casey plays baseball.
3. His great skill with the bat makes him a hero.
4. The people in the town of Mudville call him the Mighty Casey.
5. Casey is one of the greatest players.
6. He frightens pitchers.
7. He often hits the winning run for his team.
8. The fans love Casey.

B. Underline each verb or verb phrase in the past tense.

1. The game had reached the last inning.
2. The Mudville team trailed four to two.
3. The first two batters were called out at first base.
4. Many in the crowd left the game and went home.
5. But the next two men up made hits.
6. Then Casey came up to the plate.
7. The crowd went wild.

C. List four verbs you know.

	present tense	past tense
1.		
2.		
3.		
4.		

Future Tense

> ■ A verb in the **future tense** shows an action that will happen
> at some time in the future. The helping verb <u>will</u> is used
> with the present tense form of the verb.
> EXAMPLE: I **will meet** you tomorrow.

A. Write a verb in the future tense to complete each sentence.

1. Sue _____ the invitations.

2. David and Andrew _____ what games to play.

3. We all _____ the balloons with air.

4. Mary and Ella _____ the table decorations.

5. Carlos and Rosa _____ the cake.

6. Chris _____ of a way to get Tony to come over.

7. We all _____ in the back room.

8. When Chris and Tony come in, everyone _____, "Surprise!"

B. The sentences below show an event that happened in the past. Rewrite each underlined verb to change the event to a time in the future.

1. Carla <u>sent</u> a letter to the Round-the-World Travel Agency. _____will send_____

2. She <u>received</u> an answer in a day or two. _____

3. The agency <u>mailed</u> her folders containing information about exciting places to visit. _____

4. Carla <u>studied</u> the information. _____

5. She <u>chose</u> to write about three places. _____

6. Then she <u>planned</u> an imaginary trip to those three places. _____

7. She <u>wrote</u> in detail about her imaginary trip. _____

8. She <u>designed</u> her report with pictures from the travel agency folders. _____

9. She <u>made</u> an interesting cover for her report. _____

10. Then she <u>hoped</u> for a good grade. _____

Subject-Verb Agreement

- A **singular subject** must have a **singular verb**.
  EXAMPLES: Jane **lives** there. She **does walk** to school.
  She **doesn't live** near me.
- A **plural subject** must have a **plural verb**.
  EXAMPLES: Jane and her sister **live** there. They **do walk**
  to school. They **don't live** near me.
- <u>You</u> and <u>I</u> must have a plural verb.

- **Write <u>S</u> over each singular subject. Write <u>P</u> over each plural subject. Then underline the correct verb in parentheses.**

1. Many stories (tell, tells) how dogs become friends of people.

2. A story by Rudyard Kipling (say, says) that Wild Dog

   agreed to help hunt and guard in exchange for bones.

3. After that, Wild Dog (become, becomes) First Friend.

4. Many dogs never (leave, leaves) their masters.

5. In another story, a dog (doesn't, don't) leave his master's

   dead body and dies in the Arctic cold.

6. There are few people in history that (doesn't, don't)

   record the usefulness of dogs.

7. Diggings in Egypt (prove, proves) that the dog was a

   companion in ancient Egypt.

8. Bones of dogs (does, do) appear in Egyptian graves.

9. Ancient Greek vases (picture, pictures) dogs on them.

10. Today the Leader Dog organization (train, trains) dogs

    to guide people who can't see.

11. One man who can't see said, "My eyes (have, has) a wet nose."

12. A dog (does, do) have excellent hearing and smelling abilities.

13. What person (doesn't, don't) agree that a dog is a

    person's best friend?

Agreement with Linking Verbs

> - A **linking verb** is a verb that joins the subject of a sentence with a word in the predicate.
>   EXAMPLES: Bob **is** an artist. Bob **was** late.
> - A singular subject must have a singular linking verb.
>   EXAMPLES: Maria **is** a singer. Maria **was** happy.
> - A plural subject must have a plural linking verb.
>   EXAMPLES: Becky and Lynn **are** sisters. The sisters **were** happy.
> - You must have a plural linking verb.

A. Write S over each singular subject. Write P over each plural subject. Then circle the correct linking verb.

1. Tracy (is, are) a clown.

2. Her brothers (is, are) acrobats.

3. Tracy and her brothers (was, were) in a show.

4. Tracy (was, were) funny.

5. Her brothers (was, were) daring.

6. The people watching (was, were) delighted.

7. Tracy (was, were) amusing with her big red nose.

8. Tracy's brothers (was, were) high in the air on a swing.

9. (Was, Were) you ever at their show?

10. Tracy (is, are) glad that I went to see her perform.

B. Circle the correct linking verb in parentheses.

1. Ice skating (is, are) a popular winter sport today.
2. (Isn't, Aren't) there a skating rink or pond in every northern town?
3. Even in many southern towns, there (is, are) an indoor rink.
4. The discovery of ice skating (were, was) an accident.
5. An Arctic settler who slipped on a piece of bone and skidded across the ice (was, were) the inventor of the ice skate.
6. Pieces of bone attached to his feet (was, were) the first ice skates.
7. Now we (is, are) all able to enjoy his invention.
8. That (was, were) a lucky day for all ice skaters!

Forms of *Go, Do, See,* and *Sing*

> ■ Never use a helping verb with <u>went</u>, <u>did</u>, <u>saw</u>, or <u>sang</u>.
>   EXAMPLES: Sue **did** her work. Sam **went** home. Sarah
>   **sang** a song.
> ■ Always use a helping verb with <u>gone</u>, <u>done</u>, <u>seen</u>, or <u>sung</u>.
>   EXAMPLES: Sarah **has done** her work. Mary **had** not
>   **seen** me.

A. Circle the correct verb in parentheses.

1. The class members (did, done) very well on their music project.
2. Most of them had (gone, went) to extra practices.
3. They (sang, sung) at the special spring concert.
4. The class had (sang, sung) in the concert before, but they (did, done) even better this year.
5. The teacher said she had never (saw, seen) a class work so well together.
6. The teacher said they had (sang, sung) beautifully.
7. They (sang, sung) so well that she was very proud of them.
8. The week after the concert, the class (gone, went) to a music museum.
9. The trip was a reward because the class had (did, done) so well.
10. The class (saw, seen) pictures of famous musicians at the museum.
11. After they had (saw, seen) an exhibit of unusual music boxes, they wished the boxes were for sale.
12. What do you think the teacher (did, done)?
13. She took the class to a music shop she had (gone, went) to before.
14. The teacher and the shop owner had (sang, sung) together.
15. They had (gone, went) to the same music school.
16. So the class (went, gone) to this shop and saw many little musical toys.
17. In the shop they (saw, seen) many small music boxes.

B. Write the correct form of each verb in parentheses.

1. (go)   Kate has _____ to voice class.
2. (do)   She has _____ that every day for a year.
3. (see)   Her friends have _____ her sing in public.
4. (sing)   She _____ last week at the auditorium.

Forms of *Break, Drink, Take,* and *Write*

> ■ Never use a helping verb with <u>broke</u>, <u>drank</u>, <u>took</u>, or <u>wrote</u>.
>   EXAMPLES: Kim **broke** her arm. Jack **wrote** a letter.
> ■ Always use a helping verb with <u>broken</u>, <u>drunk</u>, <u>taken</u>, or <u>written</u>.
>   EXAMPLES: Kim **has broken** her arm. Jack **had written** a note.

A. Complete each sentence with the correct form of one of the verbs below.

broke, broken	drank, drunk	took, taken	wrote, written

1. Rick _____ his time writing the letter.

2. He had _____ Janet's sculpture from her, and he needed to

   apologize.

3. He _____ slowly and carefully, thinking hard about each word.

4. Whenever he paused, he _____ sips of water from the glass on
   his desk.

5. In the letter, he said he was sorry he had _____ the sculpture.

6. Although he tried to be careful, he _____ it.

7. He _____ that he would never do anything like that again.

8. Then he read what he had _____ .

9. He saw that he had _____ all of his water.

10. It had _____ all his courage to write that letter.

B. Write the correct form of each verb in parentheses.

1. (take)   Alan had _____ his dog for a long walk and was thirsty.

2. (drink)   So he had _____ a glass of fruit juice.

3. (break)   He was careful and had not _____ the glass.

4. (break)   But then his dog, Ruby, had _____ it.

5. (write)   Now Alan has _____ a note of apology.

Forms of *Eat, Draw, Give,* and *Ring*

> - Never use a helping verb with <u>ate</u>, <u>drew</u>, <u>gave</u>, or <u>rang</u>.
>   EXAMPLES: Ann **ate** her lunch. The telephone **rang.**
> - Always use a helping verb with <u>eaten</u>, <u>drawn</u>, <u>given</u>, or <u>rung</u>.
>   EXAMPLES: Ann **has eaten** her lunch. The telephone
>   **has rung.**

A. Complete each sentence with the correct form of the verb in parentheses.

1. (give) Martha _____ samples of the granola bars she had made to three of her friends.

2. (eat) The bars were soon _____, and there were cries of "More!"

3. (eat) "You _____ those already?" Martha asked.

4. (give) "I should have _____ you the recipe."

5. (eat) "Please do!" said her friends. "We have never _____ anything so delicious."

6. (give) "I _____ them to you for your health's sake," said Martha.

7. (ring) Just then the telephone _____ .

8. (draw) "Hello," said Martha. "You have _____ my name?"

9. (draw) "They _____ my name as the winner!" she told her friends.

10. (ring) "If that phone hadn't _____ when it did, we would have gone home," said Paul.

11. (eat) "If you had _____ any faster, you would have missed all the excitement," said Martha.

B. Circle the correct verb in parentheses.

1. The telephone has just (rang, rung).

2. Carla and Betty have (eat, eaten) breakfast and are looking for something to do.

3. Now Joseph has (gave, given) them a call to ask if they would like to come to his house.

Forms of *Begin, Fall, Steal,* and *Throw*

> - Never use a helping verb with <u>began</u>, <u>fell</u>, <u>stole</u>, or <u>threw</u>.
>   EXAMPLES: Sue **began** to run. José **fell** down.
> - Always use a helping verb with <u>begun</u>, <u>fallen</u>, <u>stolen</u>, or <u>thrown</u>.
>   EXAMPLES: Sue **had begun** to run. José **had fallen**.

A. Circle the correct verb in parentheses.

1. Spring baseball practice had just (began, begun).
2. The pitchers on the Blasters' team had (threw, thrown) a few balls.
3. The other Blasters (began, begun) to practice.
4. They would need much practice, because they had (fell, fallen) into last place at the end of last season.
5. The Blasters' coaches (threw, thrown) themselves into their work.
6. The biggest job (fell, fallen) on the batting and base-running coach.
7. The team batting average had (fell, fallen) out of sight.
8. And the players had (stole, stolen) only forty bases last year.
9. The coach said, "Our team motto will be 'We have just (began, begun) to fight!' "
10. With that, the Blasters (fell, fallen) to work.
11. The pitchers (threw, thrown) many different kinds of pitches.
12. The fastest pitch was (threw, thrown) at ninety miles per hour.
13. The batters were hitting everything that was (threw, thrown) to them.

B. Write the correct form of each verb in parentheses.

1. (steal) In last night's opening game, Nick, our team's fastest

   base runner, had _____ home.

2. (begin) We had _____ to warm up Willis, our relief pitcher,

   before the sixth inning.

3. (throw) He had _____ the ball so well last year that

   no batters could hit his pitches.

4. (begin) After Willis won last night's game for us, we told him that

   he had _____ our season in great style.

Subject and Object Pronouns

- A **pronoun** is a word that is used in place of a noun.
  EXAMPLES: Juan read a story. **He** enjoyed the story.
- A **subject pronoun** is a pronoun that is used as the subject of a sentence. He, I, it, she, they, we, and you are subject pronouns.
  EXAMPLES: **She** helped Joe. **I** helped, too.
- An **object pronoun** is a pronoun that is used in place of a noun that receives the action of the verb. Her, him, it, me, them, us, and you are object pronouns.
  EXAMPLES: Diane called **me**. I answered **her.**

A. Circle the subject pronoun that could be used in place of the underlined subject.

1. Susan (Her, She) saw the bus nearing the corner.
2. Joseph (Him, He) ran down the street to stop the bus.
3. The children (Them, They) saw Susan from the bus windows.
4. Ann (Her, She) called to Ms. Thomas, the driver, to wait.
5. The bus (It, He) stopped just in time.
6. Ms. Thomas (Her, She) let Susan on the bus.
7. Then Susan (her, she) waved goodbye to Joseph.
8. Susan (Her, She) was glad the bus had waited for her.

B. Circle the correct object pronoun that could be used in place of the underlined object.

1. "Tony invited Bill and (I, me) to his birthday party,"
   said Tom.
2. "He asked Tom and Bill (us, we) to be right on time,"
   Bill said.
3. "Tony's friends are giving Tony (he, him) a special gift," Tom said. "They are giving him tickets to the baseball game."
4. "They bought the tickets (them, they) last week."
5. Bill asked, "Do you think Tony's friends bought Tony, Bill, and Tom (us, we) front row seats?"
6. "Let's ask Tony's friends (them, they)," Tom answered.

Possessive Pronouns

- A **possessive pronoun** is a pronoun that shows who or what owns something.
  EXAMPLES: The shoes are **mine.** Those are **my** shoes.
- The possessive pronouns <u>hers</u>, <u>mine</u>, <u>ours</u>, <u>theirs</u>, and <u>yours</u> stand alone.
  EXAMPLES: The dog is **mine.** This book is **yours.**
- The possessive pronouns <u>her</u>, <u>its</u>, <u>my</u>, <u>our</u>, <u>their</u>, and <u>your</u> must be used before nouns.
  EXAMPLES: **Their** house is gray. **Her** cat is white.
- The pronoun <u>his</u> may be used either way.
  EXAMPLES: That is **his** car. The car is **his.**

A. Circle the possessive pronoun that completes each sentence.

1. Carol lent me (her, hers) sweater.
2. I thought that (her, hers) was warmer than mine.
3. We often trade (our, ours) jackets and sweaters.
4. I hope I don't forget which are (her, hers)
   and which are (my, mine).
5. My cousin Patty and I have the same problem with
   (our, ours) bikes.
6. Both of (our, ours) are the same make and model.
7. The only difference is that (mine, my) handlebar
   grips are blue and (her, hers) are green.
8. What kind of dog is (your, yours)?
9. (Your, Yours) dog's ears are pointed.
10. (It, Its) tail is stubby.

B. Complete each pair of sentences by writing the correct possessive pronoun.

1. Bill owns a beautiful horse named Tony.

   _____ spots are brown and white.

2. Bill has taught the horse some tricks.

   In fact, _____ horse counts with its hoof.

3. Bill's sisters have horses, too.

   Bill is going to train them for _____ sisters.

Adjectives

> - An **adjective** is a word that describes a noun or a pronoun.
>   EXAMPLE: The field is dotted with **beautiful** flowers.
> - Adjectives usually tell **what kind, which one,** or **how many.**
>   EXAMPLES: **tall** trees, the **other** hat, **five** dollars

A. In the sentences below, underline each adjective and circle the noun it describes. Some sentences may contain more than one adjective. Do not include a, an, or the.

1. The early Greeks thought a healthy body was important.
2. They believed that strong bodies meant healthy minds.
3. The Olympics began in Greece in the distant past.
4. The great god Zeus and the powerful Cronus both wanted to own Earth.
5. They battled on the high peaks of the beautiful mountains of Greece.
6. Zeus won the mighty struggle, and the first Olympics were
   held in the peaceful valley below Mount Olympus.

B. Expand the meaning of each sentence below by writing an adjective to describe each underlined noun.

1. The _____ runners from _____ nations lined up for the race.

2. Several _____ skaters competed for the _____ medal.

3. The _____ skiers sped down the _____ slopes.

4. We noticed the _____ colors of their _____ clothing against the _____ snow.

5. Hundreds of _____ fans greeted the _____ winners of each event.

6. As the _____ song of the winner's country was played, _____ tears streamed down her _____ face.

C. Fill in each blank with an adjective telling how many or which one.

1. _____ days of vacation

2. the _____ race

3. the _____ row of desks

4. _____ library books

Adjectives That Compare

- Adjectives that compare two nouns end in -er.
  EXAMPLES: Jack is **taller** than Bill. Bill is **heavier** than Jack.
- Adjectives that compare more than two nouns end in -est.
  EXAMPLE: Sam is the **tallest** and **heaviest** in the class.
- Most longer adjectives use more and most to compare.
  EXAMPLES: **more** beautiful, **most** beautiful

- **Underline the correct form of the adjective.**

1. Last year's science fair was the (bigger, biggest) one we have ever had.

2. For one thing, it had the (larger, largest) attendance ever.

3. Also, most students felt that the projects were (more interesting, most interesting) than last year's.

4. Of the two models of the solar system, Ray's was the (larger, largest).

5. However, Mary's model was (more accurate, most accurate) in scale.

6. The judges had a difficult task, but they gave the (higher, highest) rating to Mary's model.

7. Sue's, Tim's, and Becky's projects on cameras drew the (bigger, biggest) crowds at the fair.

8. These projects were the (more popular, most popular) of all.

9. Sue's project had the (prettier, prettiest) display of photographs.

10. But Becky's showed the (greater, greatest) understanding of a camera's workings.

11. Tim's project, however, was the (finer, finest) all-around project of the three.

12. One judge said, "This was the (harder, hardest) job I've ever had."

Adverbs

> - An **adverb** is a word that describes a verb. It tells **how, when, where,** or **how often** the action shown by a verb happens.
> - Many adverbs end in -ly.
>   EXAMPLES: The bell rang **loudly**. The bell rang **today**.
>   The bell rang **downstairs**. The bell rang **often**.

A. Circle each verb. Then underline each adverb that describes the verb. Next, write how, when, where, or how often.

1. Rob and Jeff (had talked) daily about visiting the empty old house.   _____how often_____

2. They often walked by it on their way to school.   _____

3. But they seldom had time to stop.   _____

4. They suddenly decided that today was the day.   _____

5. So on the way home from school, they slipped quietly through the front gate.   _____

6. They crept carefully up the creaky front steps.   _____

7. Rob quietly opened the front door.   _____

8. Jeff then peered into the darkness of the front hall.   _____

9. A draft of wind instantly swept through the house.   _____

10. The back door banged loudly.   _____

11. Rob and Jeff ran swiftly out the front door and through the gate.   _____

12. They never returned to that empty old house.   _____

B. Choose the correct adverb for each sentence.

finally   late   nervously   Suddenly

1. Dean's plane was arriving _____.

2. Nancy kept glancing _____ at the clock in the airport.

3. _____ the gate lights flashed.

4. Dean's plane _____ had landed.

Adverbs That Compare

- Add -er when using short adverbs to compare two actions.
  EXAMPLE: Joe ran **faster** than Jill.
- Add -est when using short adverbs to compare more than two actions.
  EXAMPLE: Jim ran **fastest** of all.
- Use more or most with longer adverbs and with adverbs that end in -ly when comparing two or more than two actions.
  EXAMPLES: Rob answered **more quickly** than Sue. Tim answered **most quickly** of all.

■ **Complete each sentence below by writing the correct form of the adverb shown in parentheses.**

1. (close) Amy lives _____ to Lake Hope than we do.

2. (early) She usually arrives there _____ than we do.

3. (fast) Amy says that I can row _____ than anyone else on the lake.

4. (quickly) But my cousin Jake can bait a hook _____ than I can.

5. (patiently) Amy can wait _____ than Jake and I put together.

6. (carefully) Jake and I are both careful, but Amy baits the hook _____.

7. (quietly) Jake and I try to see who can sit _____.

8. (soon) I usually break the silence _____ than Jake.

9. (skillfully) I'd have to admit that Amy fishes _____ of the three of us.

10. (happily) And no one I know welcomes us to her home _____ than she does.

Adjectives or Adverbs

> - Remember that adjectives describe nouns or pronouns.
>   Adjectives tell **what kind, which one,** or **how many.**
>   EXAMPLES: **blue** sky, **this** year, **several** pages
> - Remember that adverbs describe verbs. Adverbs tell **how,
>   when, where,** or **how often.**
>   EXAMPLES: Walk **slowly.** Go **now.** Come **here.**

- **In the sentences below, underline each adjective. Circle each adverb.**

1. Three men were given licenses to hunt once on rugged Kodiak Island.

2. They had finally received permission to hunt the wild
   animals that live there.

3. Their purpose was different than the word "hunt" usually suggests.

4. The men were zoo hunters and would try to catch
   three bear cubs.

5. The young cubs would soon have a comfortable,
   new home at a distant zoo.

6. Once on the hilly island, the hopeful men quietly
   unpacked and then lay down for six hours of rest.

7. The next day, the men carefully scanned the rocky cliffs
   through powerful glasses.

8. They saw a huge brown bear with three cubs
   tumbling playfully around her.

9. The men spent two hours climbing quietly up to a point
   overlooking that ledge.

10. A large den could barely be seen in the rocks.

11. The wise men knew that bears never charge uphill.

12. However, the human scent immediately warned the watchful
    mother bear.

13. With a fierce roar, she walked heavily out of the cave
    and stared up at the men with her beady eyes.

14. One of the men tightly tied a red bandana and a dirty
    sock to a rope and threw the bundle down the slope.

15. The curious bear charged clumsily after it.

16. Quickly the men dropped to the wide ledge below.

17. But the wise cubs successfully hid from the men.

Prepositions

> - A **preposition** is a word that shows the relationship of a noun or a pronoun to another word in the sentence.
>   EXAMPLES: The cat **under** the tree is mine.
> - Some prepositions include: <u>in</u>, <u>down</u>, <u>to</u>, <u>by</u>, <u>of</u>, <u>with</u>, <u>for</u>, and <u>at</u>.
> - A **prepositional phrase** is a group of words that begins with a preposition and ends with a noun or a pronoun.
>   EXAMPLES: **in** the house, **down** the street, **to** us

**A. Underline the prepositional phrase in each sentence below.
Circle the prepositions.**

1. The box (on) the dining room table was wrapped.
2. A friend of Marta's was having a birthday.
3. Marta had been saving money for weeks so she could buy the present.
4. Now Marta was dressing in her bedroom.
5. Marta's little sister Tina toddled into the dining room.
6. She pulled the tablecloth, and the box fell to the floor.
7. Marta heard a thump and ran to the dining room.
8. Tina hid under the table.
9. The playful look on her face made Marta smile.

B. Underline ten prepositional phrases in the paragraph below.

> When I went into the store, I looked at coats. I needed a new one to wear during the winter. I left my old one on the bus. When I got on the bus, I noticed it was very hot. I took off my coat and put it under my seat. When I got off the bus, I forgot it. When I asked about it, I was told to look at the office. It was not there.

C. Give directions for a treasure hunt. Use the prepositional phrases below in your sentences.

around the corner	near the school	under a rock	beneath the tree

_____

_____

_____

_____

Using *May/Can* and *Good/Well*

> - <u>May</u> expresses **permission.**
>   EXAMPLE: **May** I go to town?
> - <u>Can</u> expresses the **ability** to do something.
>   EXAMPLE: She **can** play well.
> - <u>Good</u> is an adjective. It tells **what kind.**
>   EXAMPLE: My sister is a **good** cook.
> - <u>Well</u> is an adverb. It tells **how.**
>   EXAMPLE: Did you do **well** today?

- **Underline the correct word in each sentence below.**

1. (Can, May) I use the pen on your desk, Sam?

2. Yes, you (can, may) use it, but I doubt that you (can, may) make it work, Sara.

3. Look, Sam! It's working (good, well) now.

4. That's (good, well). How did you make it work?

5. (Can, May) we have an early appointment, Doctor Morris?

6. Just a moment. I'll see whether I (can, may) arrange that.

7. Yes, I believe that will work out (good, well).

8. Thank you, doctor. That will be (good, well) for my schedule, too.

9. Juan, (can, may) we have these stacks of old magazines?

10. Of course you (can, may), Shelly.

11. Are you sure you (can, may) carry them, though?

12. I (can, may) help you if they are too heavy for you.

13. Thank you, Juan, but I'm sure that I (can, may) manage very (good, well).

14. That's a (good, well) money-making project you have. What is the money being used for?

15. We're raising money for new school band uniforms, and we're doing quite (good, well), too.

16. Susan did a (good, well) job on her science project.

17. She did so (good, well) that she will take her project to the state fair this summer.

18. She will also bring a guest with her, and she has a (good, well) idea who she will bring.

19. If Alan (can, may), he will do a project and go with her.

Using *Teach/Learn* and *Set/Sit*

> - <u>Teach</u> means "to give instruction to others."
>   EXAMPLE: Rosa will **teach** me to speak Spanish.
> - <u>Learn</u> means "to get knowledge."
>   EXAMPLE: I'm **learning** to speak Spanish.
> - <u>Set</u> means "to place something in a special position."
>   EXAMPLE: Please **set** the books on the table.
> - <u>Sit</u> means "to take a resting position."
>   EXAMPLE: Please **sit** down and rest for a minute.

- **Underline the correct word in each sentence below.**
  1. Andy: Who will (learn, teach) you to play the piano?
  2. Pat: I hope to (learn, teach) from my sister, Beth.
  3. Andy: Wouldn't it be better to have Ms. Hill (learn, teach) you?
  4. Pat: You were quite small when she began to (learn, teach) you.
  5. Pat: Was it hard to (learn, teach) when you were so young?
  6. Andy: Yes, but Ms. Hill let me (set, sit) on a high, round stool.
  7. Andy: At home I would (set, sit) a thick book on the piano bench
       and (set, sit) on it.
  8. Andy: Then I grew enough so that I could (set, sit) on the bench
       and still reach the keys.

  9. Liz: Beth asked Marty to (learn, teach) her how to drive.
  10. Liz: She says it would make her nervous to have someone that
        she didn't know (learn, teach) her.
  11. Tom: Are you going to go along and (set, sit) in the back seat?
  12. Liz: I doubt that Beth will want me to (set, sit) anywhere
        near when she is driving.

  13. Scott: Martha, I am going to (learn, teach) you a new skill.
  14. Scott: I know you are old enough to (learn, teach) how
        to (set, sit) the table.
  15. Scott: (Set, Sit) there, Martha, so that you can watch me.
  16. Scott: First I (set, sit) the plates in their places.
  17. Scott: Then I put a glass at each place where someone will (set, sit).
  18. Scott: Once I (learn, teach) you everything, you will be able
        to (set, sit) the table every night.
  19. Martha: Good! Let me try to (set, sit) it now.

Unit 3 Test

Choose the correct plural form of each underlined noun.

1. buggy

   A ○ buggys   **C** ○ buggies

   B ○ buggyes   **D** ○ buggeys

2. man

   A ○ manes   **C** ○ mans

   B ○ mens   **D** ○ men

3. box

   A ○ boxs   **C** ○ boxies

   B ○ boxes   **D** ○ boxss

4. shelf

   A ○ shelves   **C** ○ shelvs

   B ○ shelfs   **D** ○ shelfes

Choose the correct possessive form of each underlined noun.

5. Maria

   A ○ Marias   **C** ○ Marias's

   B ○ Marias'   **D** ○ Maria's

6. child

   A ○ childs'   **C** ○ child's

   B ○ childrens'   **D** ○ childs's

7. house

   A ○ house's   **C** ○ hous's

   B ○ houses'   **D** ○ housse

8. heroes

   A ○ heroe's   **C** ○ hero'es

   B ○ heroes'   **D** ○ heros'

Choose the correct answer to each question.

9. In which sentence is an action verb underlined?

   A ○ We planned a picnic.

   B ○ But each week it has rained.

   C ○ Now the sun is out.

   D ○ I hope it is sunny this weekend.

10. In which sentence is a helping verb underlined?

   A ○ Mary has an Irish wolfhound.

   B ○ I have seen it.

   C ○ At first I was afraid.

   D ○ But I find the dog is gentle.

Choose the sentence that contains a correct verb form of the verb tense shown.

11. past tense

   A ○ We knew what had happened.

   B ○ We known it would happen.

   C ○ We know how things happen.

   D ○ We will know when it happens.

12. future tense

   A ○ I went to the seashore.

   B ○ I will go to the seashore.

   C ○ I have gone to the seashore.

   D ○ I go to the seashore.

Choose the correct verb to complete each sentence.

13. Brenda and Gary _____ helping.

   A ○ was   **C** ○ were

   B ○ is   **D** ○ am

14. The truck _____ in the ditch.

   A ○ were   **C** ○ is

   B ○ am   **D** ○ are

15. Iris _____ the wrong turn.

   A ○ took   **C** ○ has took

   B ○ taken **D** ○ take

16. She _____ three books.

   A ○ write   **C** ○ had wrote

   B ○ has wrote **D** ○ has written

Choose the correct answer to each question.

17. In which sentence is the object pronoun underlined?

   A ○ She waved hello to Mrs. Martelli.

   B ○ They told him to go.

   C ○ Randy's tie was too long.

   D ○ Jerry and Ned spoke quietly.

18. In which sentence is the possessive pronoun underlined?

   A ○ Its handle had broken.

   B ○ No one had known about it before.

   C ○ Watch out for them.

   D ○ The people walked by slowly.

19. In which sentence is the subject pronoun underlined?

   A ○ They invited us to a party.

   B ○ Kathy could not go to it.

   C ○ Some dogs and cats like each other.

   D ○ They are not friendly.

20. In which sentence is the adjective underlined?

   A ○ The sky was brightly shining.

   B ○ Clouds floated across the blue sky.

   C ○ Patrick smiled happily at his brother.

   D ○ Don't get too upset with them.

Choose the word that is used as a preposition in each sentence.

21. You didn't tell him to go into the cave.

   A ○ our   **C** ○ into

   B ○ not   **D** ○ that

22. We had a great time at the beach.

   A ○ we   **C** ○ time

   B ○ at   **D** ○ the

Choose the sentence that is correct.

23. **A** ○ Can I have the mustard?

   B ○ I did good today at work.

   C ○ May I borrow that magazine?

   D ○ Are you sure you may lift that?

24. **A** ○ Learn me how to play the piano.

   B ○ Set it down on the table.

   C ○ That was a well book.

   D ○ He sit his plate in the sink.

25. **A** ○ I hope you feel well today.

   B ○ He learned her the first verse.

   C ○ Todd may sing good.

   D ○ I will teach how by myself.

26. **A** ○ It was well we went to see him.

   B ○ The sun sit slowly in the west.

   C ○ I will teach you to do that.

   D ○ We can fix that very good.

Capitalizing First Words

- **Capitalize** the first word of a sentence.
  - EXAMPLE: Many people have pen pals.
- Capitalize the first word of a direct quotation.
  - EXAMPLE: Jane asked, "Where does your pen pal live?"

A. Circle each letter that should be capitalized. Write the capital letter above it.

1. "have you met your pen pal?" I asked.

2. john answered, "yes, he spent the holidays with me."

3. so I've invited my pen pal to visit me.

4. he hopes to arrive in my country next June.

5. i am making many plans for his visit.

6. we're going to hike in the mountains.

- Capitalize the first word of every line of poetry.
  - EXAMPLE: There was a monkey climbed up a tree;
    When he fell down, then down fell he.
- Capitalize the first, last, and all important words in the titles of books, poems, stories, and songs.
  - EXAMPLE: Who wrote *Little House on the Prairie?*

B. Circle each letter that should be capitalized. Write the capital letter above it.

1. there was an old woman

   lived under a hill,

   and if she's not gone,

   she lives there still.

2. if all the world were water,

   and all the water were ink,

   what should we do for bread and cheese?

   and what should we do for drink?

3. Have you read Longfellow's poem "the song of hiawatha"?

4. We are learning the song "down by the river."

5. If you're interested in ballooning, read *up, up and away.*

6. Mike wrote a story called "a balloon ride."

Capitalizing Proper Nouns and Adjectives

> ■ Capitalize all proper nouns.
>   EXAMPLES: Main Street, Germany, Atlantic Ocean, Friday,
>   Florida, Rocky Mountains, Halloween, December, Aunt Ann,
>   Mom, Holmes School, James
> ■ A proper adjective is an adjective that is made from a
>   proper noun. Capitalize all proper adjectives.
>   EXAMPLES: the English language, Italian dishes, French
>   people, American tourists, the Australian cities

**A. Circle each letter that should be capitalized. Write the capital letter
above it.**

1. My friend larry had just returned from a world trip.

2. He brought gifts for everyone in my family, including my

   dog, chipper.

3. He gave my mother some delicate japanese dishes that he

   bought in tokyo, japan.

4. He gave my sister a scottish plaid kilt like the bagpipers

   wear in scotland.

5. My father really likes the hat larry got for him in london.

6. The hat reminds us of the kind sherlock holmes wore.

7. My gift was an african drum from mali in west africa.

8. larry told us how delicious the italian food was.

9. chipper's gift was a colorful, embroidered dog jacket

   from thailand.

**B. Write four sentences about a trip you would like to take.
Use proper nouns and at least one proper adjective in the sentences.**

1. _____

2. _____

3. _____

4. _____

Capitalizing Titles and Abbreviations

- Capitalize a person's title when it comes before a name.
  - EXAMPLES: Mayor Thomas, Governor Swanson
- Capitalize abbreviations of titles.
  - EXAMPLES: Dr. Norris; Mr. and Mrs. J. B. Benton, Jr.; Ms. Harris; Mr. John F. Lynch, Sr.

A. Circle each letter that should be capitalized. Write the capital letter above it.

1. We saw governor potter and senator williams in their offices.

2. They were discussing a national health problem with dr. laura bedford and mayor phillips.

3. We ate lunch with rev. barton and mr. james adams, jr.

4. They are part of a committee planning a welcome for prince charles of England, who will tour our state next month.

- Capitalize abbreviations of days and months, parts of addresses, and titles of members of the armed forces. Also capitalize all letters in abbreviations for states.
  - EXAMPLES: Mon.; Sept.; 501 N. Elm St.; Capt. W. R. Russell; Chicago, IL

B. Circle each letter that should be capitalized. Write the capital letter above it.

1. gen. david e. morgan

   6656 n. second ave.

   evanston, il 60202

2. valentine's day Exhibit

   at oak grove library

   mon.—fri., feb 10—14

   101 e. madison st.

3. sgt. carlos m. martinez

   17 watling st.

   shropshire SY7 0LW, england

4. maxwell school Field Day

   wed., apr. 30, 1:00

   Register mon.—tues., apr. 28—29

   mr. modica's office

Using End Punctuation

> - Use a **period** at the end of a declarative sentence.
>   EXAMPLE: The lens is an important part of a camera.
> - Use a **question mark** at the end of an interrogative sentence.
>   EXAMPLE: Do you enjoy having your picture taken?

A. Add the correct end punctuation to each sentence below.

1. Photography is an exciting hobby for many people
2. My friend Karen is one of those people
3. Have you ever gone on a vacation with a camera bug
4. Craig and I love Karen's photos
5. But getting those really good shots can be tiring
6. Can you imagine waiting in the hot desert sun while Karen
   gets just the right angle on a cactus
7. Or have you ever sat in the car while your friend waited
   for a grazing elk to turn its head
8. I don't need so much time when I take pictures
9. Of course my pictures aren't always as good as Karen's

B. Add the correct end punctuation where needed in the paragraphs below.

Have you ever wondered what it would be like to live as
our country's pioneers did___ You can visit log homes made to
look like the original cabins of pioneer days___ Then you can
see how difficult life was for the pioneers who helped our
country grow___

The cabins were small and roughly built___ Many cabins had
just one room___ Where was the kitchen___ Most of the cooking was
done in the large fireplace___ The fireplace also supplied the
only heat___ Wasn't it cold___ You can be sure the winter winds
whistled between the logs___ And where did the pioneers sleep___
Most cabins had a ladder reaching up to the bedroom loft___

The furniture in the cabins was usually as roughly built as
the cabins themselves___ All the clothing was handmade by the
family___ They ate food grown and caught on their land___ Would
you have liked to live in those times___

■ Use a period at the end of an imperative sentence.
  EXAMPLE: Please sign your name here.
■ Use an **exclamation point** at the end of an exclamatory sentence.
  EXAMPLE: What a wonderful time we had at the show!

C. Add the correct end punctuation to each sentence below.

1. A group of friends decided to go ice skating___
2. Terry asked, "Is Thursday okay with all of you___"
3. Carmen said, "It sounds great to me___"
4. They all agreed to meet at the lake___
5. Elaine said, "Wow, is it ever cold___"
6. "Get moving," said Leon. "You'll warm right up___"
7. They skated for several hours___
8. Terry asked, "Who's ready to sit close to a warm fire___"
9. Carmen said, "I thought you'd never ask___"
10. Suddenly she was hit by a snowball___
11. "Hey___" she shouted. "What's the big idea___"
12. Elaine laughed and said, "It's not that cold out___"

D. Add the correct end punctuation where needed in the paragraphs below.

Have you ever seen pictures of northern Minnesota___ It is a region of many lakes___ My family once spent a week on Little Birch Lake___ What a sight it was___

There were thousands of white birches reflected in the blue water___ The fishing was great___ Every day we caught large numbers of bass, and every night we cooked fresh fish for our dinner___

The nearest town was Hackensack___ At the waterfront was a large statue of Diana Marie Kensack___ She is seated at the water's edge___ Her gaze is fixed on the horizon___ Do you know who she was___ Legends say that she was Paul Bunyan's sweetheart___ She is still waiting at the shore for him to come back to her___ Be sure to visit Diana when you are in Minnesota___

Using Quotation Marks

> - Use **quotation marks** to show the exact words of a speaker. Use a comma or other punctuation marks to separate the quotation from the rest of the sentence.
>   EXAMPLE: "Who made this delicious candy?" asked Claire.
> - A quotation may be placed at the beginning or the end of a sentence. It may also be divided within the sentence.
>   EXAMPLES: Lawrence said, "Let's play checkers."
>   "My brother," said Leslie, "brought me this ring."

A. Add quotation marks to each sentence below.

1. We will read about a great inventor today, said Miss Davis.

2. Let me see, Miss Davis went on, whether you can guess who the inventor is.

3. Will you give us some clues? asked Chris.

4. Yes, answered Miss Davis, and here is the first clue.

5. His inventions have made our lives easier and more pleasant, said Miss Davis.

6. Is it Alexander Graham Bell? asked Judy.

7. Mr. Bell did give us the telephone, said Miss Davis, but he is not the man I have in mind.

8. This man gave us another kind of machine that talks, Miss Davis said.

9. It must be Thomas Alva Edison and the phonograph, said Jerry.

10. You are right, Miss Davis said.

B. Place quotation marks and other punctuation where needed in the sentences below.

1. Polly asked Where will you spend the holidays, Michelle?

2. We plan to drive to Henry's ranch said Michelle.

3. Polly asked Won't it be quite cold?

4. Yes said Michelle but it will be so much fun to slide down the hill behind the house.

5. It's great fun to go into the woods and cut down a Christmas tree added Bob.

6. Come with us said Michelle.

Using Apostrophes

> - Use an **apostrophe** in a contraction to show where a letter or letters have been taken out.
>   EXAMPLE: I **can't** be there until three o'clock.
> - Use an apostrophe to form a possessive noun. Add -'s to most singular nouns. Add -' to most plural nouns.
>   EXAMPLE: Mike's gym shoes are high tops. The men's suits are blue and white.

- **Write the word or words in which an apostrophe has been left out. Insert the apostrophe.**

1. Building a new homes the dream of many people.   _____home's_____

2. It can also become a persons worst nightmare.   _____

3. Cant you see that planning carefully is the key?   _____

4. If you dont plan everything, somethings bound to
   go wrong.   _____

5. Youd better start by finding out how many rooms
   youll need.   _____

6. An architects view may also be helpful.   _____

7. Getting many opinions can help you decide whats best.   _____

8. But youd better already have some idea before you
   begin, or you'll have problems.   _____

9. Find out everyones wishes for their rooms.   _____

10. Others ideas may be completely different from your own. _____

11. If you talk it over, everyones ideas can be used.   _____

12. You wouldnt want to end up with a home youre
    completely unhappy with.   _____

13. After all, your homes the place where youll be spending
    most of your time.   _____

Using Commas in Sentences

> ■ Use a **comma** between words or word groups in a series.
>   EXAMPLE: Food, medical supplies, blankets, and clothing were rushed to the flooded area.
> ■ Use a comma to separate the parts of a compound sentence.
>   EXAMPLE: Many homes were flooded, and the owners were taken to safety in boats.

A. Add commas where needed in the sentences below.

1. The heavy rain caused flooding in Cedarville Taylorville Gardner and other towns along the Cedar River.

2. The flood washed away bridges roads and some small homes.

3. Our home had water in the basement and most of our neighbors' homes did, too.

4. We spent the night bailing mopping and worrying.

5. We put our washer and dryer up on blocks and then we helped Elaine.

6. Some of our shrubs flowers and small trees may have to be replaced.

7. Elaine's newly-planted vegetable garden was washed away and the Smiths lost their shed.

8. The people in our neighborhood were very lucky and everyone agreed that the flood brought us closer together.

> ■ Use a comma to separate a direct quotation from the rest of a sentence.
>   EXAMPLE: "We're leaving now," said Ann. Ann said, "It's time to go."

B. Add commas where needed in the sentences below.

1. Sally asked "Why did the rooster cross the road?"

2. "To get to the other side " answered Terry.

3. "That's really an old joke " Terry added.

4. Sally asked "Do you know a newer one?"

5. Terry asked "What holds the moon up?"

6. "Moon beams " said Terry.

> ■ Use a comma to set off the name of a person who is addressed.
>   EXAMPLE: "Alan, can't you go with us?" asked Bill.
> ■ Use a comma to set off words like <u>yes</u>, <u>no</u>, <u>well</u>, and <u>oh</u> when they begin a sentence.
>   EXAMPLE: "No, I have to visit my aunt," answered Alan.

C. Add commas where needed in the sentences below.

1. "Melody and Tim would you like to go to the hockey game?" Marie asked.
2. "Oh yes!" Tim exclaimed.
3. "Marie I'd love to," called Melody.
4. "Well it's settled," said Marie.
5. "Ted did you go to the model show last night?" asked Sam.
6. "No I couldn't make it," answered Ted.
7. "Oh I was going to ask if Carlos won a prize," Sam said.
8. "Well I hope so," Ted said.
9. "Well then," Sam said, "let's call and ask him."
10. "Carlos did you win a prize last night?" Sam asked.
11. "Yes I did," replied Carlos.
12. "Oh what did you win?" asked Sam.
13. "Well you'd never guess," answered Carlos.
14. "Carlos don't keep us guessing," said Sam.
15. "Well you know my model was of a helicopter. My prize was a ride in a helicopter!" exclaimed Carlos.

D. Pretend that you and your friends are planning an outing. Write a conversation that might take place between you and your friends. Use the names of the persons being addressed. In some sentences, use <u>yes</u>, <u>no</u>, <u>oh</u>, or <u>well</u>. Punctuate your sentences correctly.

_____

_____

_____

_____

_____

_____

_____

Unit 4 Test

Choose the word in each sentence that should be capitalized.

1. we will take our vacation to the mountains in June.
   - **A** ○ we
   - **B** ○ our
   - **C** ○ vacation
   - **D** ○ mountains

2. Have you read *Treasure island*, the exciting adventure story?
   - **A** ○ read
   - **B** ○ island
   - **C** ○ adventure
   - **D** ○ story

3. Your friend judy likes the books that author has written.
   - **A** ○ friend
   - **B** ○ judy
   - **C** ○ books
   - **D** ○ author

4. My friend likes to read poetry written by japanese poets.
   - **A** ○ friend
   - **B** ○ poetry
   - **C** ○ japanese
   - **D** ○ poets

5. Have you read governor Palmer's book about his life?
   - **A** ○ you
   - **B** ○ governor
   - **C** ○ book
   - **D** ○ life

6. The english language is spoken in many countries.
   - **A** ○ english
   - **B** ○ language
   - **C** ○ spoken
   - **D** ○ countries

7. The letter was mailed yesterday to 478 s. Baker Street.
   - **A** ○ letter
   - **B** ○ s.
   - **C** ○ mailed
   - **D** ○ yesterday

8. When did you see mrs. Webb and her children?
   - **A** ○ you
   - **B** ○ mrs.
   - **C** ○ her
   - **D** ○ children

9. sara and I are going to the museum tomorrow.
   - **A** ○ sara
   - **B** ○ going
   - **C** ○ museum
   - **D** ○ tomorrow

10. We want to see the Harry s. Truman exhibit.
    - **A** ○ want
    - **B** ○ see
    - **C** ○ s.
    - **D** ○ exhibit

Choose the sentence in which commas are used correctly.

11. **A** ○ I served fruit milk and cheese.
    B ○ Julia Billy and Mark, like fruit.
    C ○ Julia had apples, bananas, and milk.
    D ○ Sue had cheese, grapes, and, milk.

12. **A** ○ Jan, and I heard about a new show.
    B ○ Mary called and, asked us to go.
    C ○ I'd like to go today, but Jan can't.
    D ○ We want to wait and, go together.

13. **A** ○ Bears, and wolves live in the wild.
    B ○ Wildlife today, is in danger.
    C ○ Hunters shoot, many wild animals.
    D ○ Bears, wolves, and other animals should be saved.

14. **A** ○ It rained hard, and then it stopped.
    B ○ The clouds, and fog, went away.
    C ○ Sunshine dried the grass, and sidewalks.
    D ○ It was too dark, to go for a walk.

In which sentence are quotation marks used correctly?

15. A ○ "We're leaving now, said Melinda."
    B ○ "Do we have to go?" Juan asked.
    C ○ Yes, we do," Melinda answered.
    D ○ "You will have a good time.

17. A ○ "What is the point? asked Bill.
    B ○ "Well," said Paula, I don't know."
    C ○ "Who can tell us?" asked Bill.
    D ○ "Paula said, Let's ask Michael."

16. A ○ "Hello," said Jim. How are you?"
    B ○ "I'm fine, answered Joe."
    C ○ "Joe, said Jim, are you ready"?
    D ○ "No," said Joe, "I'm not."

18. A ○ Don't eat that!" cried Alice.
    B ○ "You scared me to death, said Luis.
    C ○ "Don't you know that's for dinner?
    D ○ "No, I thought it was for me!"

In which sentence is end punctuation used correctly?

19. A ○ I remember our trip to Montana?
    B ○ Bill had just learned to drive.
    C ○ Wasn't he a good driver.
    D ○ What a great time we had?

21. A ○ May I ask you a question.
    B ○ Go ahead?
    C ○ Why did you move here!
    D ○ I wanted to see a new place.

20. A ○ What a game we just saw?
    B ○ What was so good about it.
    C ○ We won!
    D ○ Shall we play tomorrow.

22. A ○ Aren't you happy now.
    B ○ Yes, I am?
    C ○ This is fantastic!
    D ○ Don't you just want me to try.

In which sentence are apostrophes used correctly?

23. A ○ I cant' believe you said that.
    B ○ We've been over this before.
    C ○ Why do'nt you understand?
    D ○ Il'I explain it again.

25. A ○ Hed' better not do that.
    B ○ And whol'l tell him?
    C ○ I'll do it.
    D ○ Okay, that way hes' safe.

24. A ○ They're on the way now.
    B ○ Its' been a long time.
    C ○ Wev'e missed seeing them.
    D ○ Im sure theyv'e been busy.

26. A ○ Taras' house is beautiful.
    B ○ It was her husband's plan.
    C ○ Their houses' front porch is huge.
    D ○ Their childrens' rooms are, too.

Writing Sentences

> ■ Every sentence has a base. The **sentence base** is made up of a simple subject and a simple predicate.
>   EXAMPLE: <u>Men</u> <u>stared</u>.
> ■ Add other words to the sentence base to expand the meaning of the sentence.
>   EXAMPLE: The **bewildered** men stared **in amazement at the mysterious light.**

A. Expand the meaning of each sentence base below. Add adjectives, adverbs, and/or prepositional phrases. Write your expanded sentence.

1. (Plane flew.) _____

2. (Creatures ran.) _____

3. (Dogs played.) _____

4. (Police chased.) _____

5. (Boys discovered.) _____

B. Imagine two different scenes for each sentence base below. Write an expanded sentence to describe each scene you imagine.

1. (Children explored.)   a. _____

   b. _____

2. (Fire was set.)   a. _____

   b. _____

3. (Crowd roared.)   a. _____

   b. _____

4. (Wind blew.)   a. _____

   b. _____

5. (Friend sent.)   a. _____

   b. _____

6. (Actor was dressed.)   a. _____

   b. _____

Name _____ Date _____

Writing Topic Sentences

> ■ A **topic sentence** is a sentence that states the main idea of
> a paragraph.   EXAMPLE: **Many of the best things in life
> are free.** The sun and the moon give their light without
> charge. A true friend can't be bought. The beauty of the
> clouds in a blue sky is there for all to enjoy.

A. Write a topic sentence for each of the paragraphs below.

1.   The summer had been extremely hot and dry. Many brush fires
had broken out. People were told not to water their lawns or wash
their cars. People responded by using less water and being
careful about how they used water. Everyone realized the new
rules were in the best interest of everyone.

TOPIC SENTENCE: _____

2.   Nancy read everything she could find about nursing. She spent
hours in the library learning about first aid. When the call came
for summer volunteers at the hospital, she was the first to sign
up. She was determined to prepare herself as best she could for
what she hoped would be her career.

TOPIC SENTENCE: _____

3.   There are many parks to enjoy. Museums and aquariums have
interesting exhibits. Large stores and malls have a great
selection of things to buy. Many large cities also have major
sports teams to watch.

TOPIC SENTENCE: _____

**B. Choose one of the topics below. Write a topic sentence for it. Then
write a paragraph of about fifty words in which you develop the topic.**

The most useful invention   My favorite holiday

A frightening experience   A place I want to visit

_____

_____

_____

_____

_____

_____

Writing Supporting Details

- Sentences that contain **supporting details** develop the topic sentence of a paragraph. The details may be facts, examples, or reasons.

A. **Read the topic sentence below. Then read the numbered sentences. Underline the four sentences that contain details that support the topic sentence.**

TOPIC SENTENCE: Automobile seat belts save lives.

1. The first seat belts didn't have shoulder straps.
2. A seat belt helps keep a front-seat passenger from going through the windshield.
3. A passenger who doesn't fasten his or her seat belt may be hurt if the car is in an accident.
4. Seat belts protect small children from falls and bumps while riding in the back seat.
5. Some cars today have automatic seat belts.
6. Studies on the number of lives saved prove the value of wearing seat belts.

B. **Underline the correct word to complete the sentence.**

The supporting details in the sentences above were (facts, examples, reasons).

C. **Choose one of the topic sentences. Write it on the first line. Then write three sentences that contain supporting details. The details may be facts, examples, or reasons.**

1. Having a pet is a lot of work.
2. A large (or small) family has advantages.
3. My vacation (in the mountains, at camp, on the seashore, or other place) was fun.
4. Every student should have an allowance.

_____

_____

_____

_____

D. **Fill in the blank below with the word facts, examples, or reasons.**

The supporting details in my paragraph were _____.

Comparing and Contrasting

> - **Comparing** two objects, persons, or ideas shows the likenesses between them. Comparing expresses a thought in a colorful, interesting way.
>   EXAMPLE: Walking lets the walker be as free as a bird that has flown from its cage.
> - **Contrasting** two objects, persons, or ideas shows the differences between them. Contrasting can also express a thought in a colorful, interesting way.
>   EXAMPLE: Baby Rachel's morning mood is one of sunshine, rainbows, and laughter. Her nap-time mood, however, suggests gathering clouds.

A. Read each topic sentence and the pair of sentences that follow. Underline the sentence that expresses a supporting detail in a colorful, interesting way.

1. TOPIC SENTENCE: Having the flu is no fun.
   a. Pat was tired of being in bed with the flu.
   b. After a week in bed with the flu, Pat felt like her pet hamster, Hamby, spinning his wheel in his cage.

2. TOPIC SENTENCE: Koalas aren't all they seem to be.
   a. A koala is cute but unfriendly.
   b. A koala looks like a cuddly teddy bear, but it is about as friendly as a grizzly bear.

B. Rewrite each sentence below in a more colorful, interesting way. Use comparison or contrast.

1. A mosquito bite is itchy.

   _____

2. Taking a bus to a museum is fun.

   _____

3. Dogs are friendlier than cats.

   _____

4. Reading is a good way to spend your free time.

   _____

5. Stealing a base makes baseball exciting.

   _____

Using Location

> ■ Supporting details can be arranged in order of location.
>   EXAMPLE: The sofa was **on the long wall to your right.**
> A table sat **at either end** of the sofa.

A. In the paragraph below, underline the words that show location.

       I stood watching. <u>Below me</u> was the ball field. Across the street from the ball field, men were building an apartment house. Cement trucks were lined up along the street. They were delivering concrete for the basement walls of the apartment house. A kindergarten class was playing baseball on the ball field. The wise teacher told the class to move away from the street.

B. Choose one of the scenes or objects below. Write a topic sentence about it. Then write a paragraph of at least five sentences describing the scene or object. Use words such as <u>above</u>, <u>ahead</u>, <u>around</u>, <u>behind</u>, <u>next to</u>, <u>on top of</u>, and <u>under</u> to show location.

       Scenes: your street, your home, a garden

       Objects: your bicycle, a car, your favorite book

_____

_____

_____

_____

_____

_____

_____

_____

_____

_____

C. Underline the words you used to show location.

Topic and Audience

> - The **topic** of a paragraph should be something the writer is interested in or familiar with.
>   EXAMPLES: school, animals, science, sports, hobbies
> - The **title** should be based on the topic.
> - The **audience** is the person or people who will read what is written.
>   EXAMPLES: classmates, readers of the class newspaper, family members

A. Suppose that the topic chosen is <u>sports</u>. Underline the sports topic below which you would most like to write about.

1. Is winning the most important thing in sports?
2. There are many reasons why tennis (or baseball, or swimming, or ____) is my favorite sport.
3. Sports can be an enjoyable family activity.

B. Think about the topic you underlined in Exercise A. Underline the audience below that you would like to write for.

1. your family
2. a coach
3. your best friend

C. Write a paragraph of about seventy words, using the sentence you underlined in Exercise A as your topic sentence. Write a title for your paragraph. Direct your paragraph to the audience you underlined in Exercise B.

_____

_____

_____

_____

_____

_____

Name _____   Date _____

Clustering

> - **Clustering** uses a special drawing that shows how ideas
>   relate to one main topic. That topic is written in a center
>   shape. Other shapes contain the ideas. Lines show how the
>   ideas are connected to the main topic.
>   EXAMPLE:
>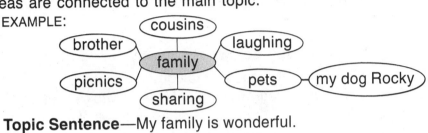
>   **Topic Sentence**—My family is wonderful.

A. Complete each cluster below by writing words that the topic makes you
think of. You may add additional shapes and connecting lines.

1.

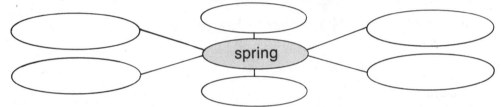

TOPIC SENTENCE: _____

2.

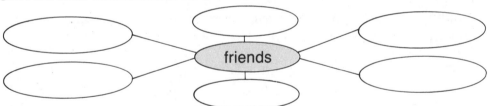

TOPIC SENTENCE: _____

B. Choose one of the topics in Exercise A. Write it on the title line below.
Then write your topic sentence for that topic. Complete the paragraph.

_____

_____

_____

_____

_____

_____

_____

Name _____ Date _____

A Descriptive Paragraph

> - A **descriptive paragraph** describes something. It is made colorful and interesting through the use of details.
>   EXAMPLE: A **thick coating** of dust covered everything in the **old abandoned** house.

A. Read the descriptive paragraph below. Then answer the question.

In my neighborhood, there is a small grocery store just a block from my house. A retired couple, Mr. and Mrs. Aggens, are the owners. I always hope that Mrs. Aggens will wait on me. She is friendly and full of smiles. She always gives me extra large scoops of ice cream. She doesn't hurry me when I can't decide whether to spend my money on apples or fruit bars. After I make my purchase, I like to stay, smell the freshly ground coffee, and talk to Mrs. Aggens.

1. What kind of person is Mrs. Aggens? Underline the words that describe her.

crabby, patient, impatient, kind, stingy, generous

B. Read the paragraph below about the same store.

In my neighborhood, there is a store near our house. The owners are a husband and wife. The wife is patient, generous, and friendly. Near the door is a fruit counter and an ice cream counter. I often shop there.

1. List at least five details that are missing from this paragraph. _____

_____

_____

2. What is the result of leaving out these details? _____

_____

C. Write a descriptive paragraph about a place you visit often. Use details to make your paragraph colorful and interesting.

_____

_____

_____

_____

Writing a Descriptive Paragraph

- Writers use **descriptive words** that tell how something looks, feels, smells, tastes, or sounds.
  EXAMPLE: The **shady** forest was dressed in the **soft greens** and **pale yellows** of early spring.
- Writers use verbs that tell exactly what someone is doing or how someone moves.
  EXAMPLE: Richard **tramped** across the newly mopped kitchen floor.

A. Read the paragraph below, and answer the questions that follow.

Jody stood silently at the rickety gate of Harry's weathered old ranch house. The crooked gate hung on only its top hinge. The house that had never known a paintbrush seemed to have whitened with age. A gentle breeze rippled the tall grass and filled Jody's nostrils with the sugary smell of sweet peas. Jody turned. Yes, there were those lovely white, pastel pink, and lavender blooms. But everything else had faded with age.

1. What words tell how the ranch house looked? _____

   how the gate looked? _____

2. What word tells how the breeze felt? _____

   how the grass looked? _____   how it moved? _____

   how the sweet peas smelled? _____   how they looked? _____

B. Choose a familiar place to write about in a descriptive paragraph. Write a topic sentence to begin the paragraph. Think about how the place looks, the sounds you might hear there, the smells you might smell there, how it feels to be there, and the things you might taste there. Write descriptive sentences that tell about these things to complete your paragraph.

_____

_____

_____

_____

_____

_____

Revising and Proofreading

- **Revising** gives you a chance to rethink and review what you have written and to improve your writing. Revise by adding words and information, by deleting unneeded words and information, and by moving words, sentences, and paragraphs around.
- **Proofreading** involves checking spelling, punctuation, grammar, and capitalization. Use proofreader's marks to show changes needed.

Proofreader's Marks

═ Capitalize.	⊙ Add a period.	⑤ᴾ Correct spelling.
/ Make a small letter.	∧ Add something.	¶ Indent for new paragraph.
⋏ Add a comma.	✗ Take something out.	⤻ Move something.

A. Rewrite the paragraphs below. Correct the errors by using the proofreader's marks.

¶ during the history of Earth there have been several ice ages these were times when giant sheets of ice spred across many parts of earth. People think that almost one third of the Land was covered by these hug sheets of ice.

The last ice age frozed so so much ocean water that the level of the oceans dropped. then lots of land apeared that usually lay underwater When the tempeture began to warm up the ice sheets melted. The Ocean levels rose again.

_____

_____

_____

_____

_____

_____

_____

Name _____   Date _____

Unit 5 Test

Read the paragraph. Then choose the correct answer to each question.

Most American newspapers have a separate section for sports news. Many people even read the sports section first. Sports magazines are also very popular. Television and radio cover sporting events almost daily. Crowds fill our stadiums and parks. Many fans stand for hours to buy tickets. Others buy season tickets so they can watch their favorite team often.

1. Which sentence could best be a topic sentence for the paragraph above?

    A ○ My favorite sport is baseball.

    B ○ *Sports Illustrated* magazine covers many different sports.

    C ○ Americans show a tremendous interest in sports.

    D ○ Many Americans are athletic.

2. Which sentence would not be a supporting detail for this paragraph?

    A ○ Some American magazines cover just one sport, in detail.

    B ○ Many Americans watch the Olympics.

    C ○ I read a good magazine last night.

    D ○ Many people collect athletes' autographs.

3. What is the purpose of a topic sentence?

    A ○ to give an opinion

    B ○ to state the main idea of a paragraph

    C ○ to support the main idea of a paragraph

    D ○ to introduce the writer

4. Which audience would not be interested in the paragraph above?

    A ○ coaches

    B ○ teenagers

    C ○ babies

    D ○ adults

Choose the correct answer to each question.

5. Which is a descriptive word?

    A ○ and   C ○ crabby

    B ○ so   D ○ is

6. Which sentence uses comparison to describe?

    A ○ I like to play baseball.

    B ○ My brother is a very good swimmer.

    C ○ Hang gliding makes people feel as free as a bird.

    D ○ Our team won the relay race.

7. What is a title based on?

    A ○ topic   C ○ location

    B ○ contrast   D ○ comparison

8. Which words would be used often in a paragraph using location?

    A ○ taste, smell, sound

    B ○ itchy, gentle, harsh

    C ○ swim, dive, pool

    D ○ above, behind, next to

Read the paragraph. Then choose the correct answer to each question.

    Language is a set of written or spoken symbols used to communicate. It is a powerful tool. Language lets parents teach their children. It gives people a way to share what they know and what they do. Language allows people to write down their experiences and feelings through writing. These written records let people pass on their skills and knowledge.

9. Which sentence could best be a topic sentence for the paragraph above?

    A ○ People from different countries speak different languages.

    B ○ People use language to communicate with each other.

    C ○ People can speak with words and with hand motions.

    D ○ Reading teaches people what others know.

10. Which sentence would be a supporting detail for this paragraph?

    A ○ Working with tools is another skill people have.

    B ○ Animals do not have a common language.

    C ○ Knowledge is what people know.

    D ○ All humans talk to each other in some way.

Choose the correct answer to each question.

11. Which proofreader's mark means to add something?

    A ○ ∧

    B ○ ⊙

    C ○ ℘

    D ○ ⌒↘

12. Which proofreader's mark means to move something?

    A ○ ⊙

    B ○ ℘

    C ○ ⌒→

    D ○ ¶

13. Which proofreader's mark means to take something out?

    A ○ ⌒↘

    B ○ ⊙

    C ○ ¶

    D ○ ℘

14. Which proofreader's mark means to capitalize?

    A ○ /

    B ○ ⊙

    C ○ ≡

    D ○ ¶

15. Which proofreader's mark means to add a period?

    A ○ ∧

    B ○ ⊙

    C ○ ℘

    D ○ /

16. Which proofreader's mark means to make a small letter?

    A ○ ∧

    B ○ /

    C ○ ≡

    D ○ ⊙

Following Directions

■ When following written **directions**, it is important to read each step carefully. Be sure you have completed one step before going on to the next step.

■ **Read the recipe below. Then answer the questions that follow it.**

Peanut Butter Balls

½ cup wheat germ   ½ cup powdered milk
½ cup sunflower seeds   ½ cup honey
½ cup peanut butter   ½ cup sesame seeds (if desired)

a. Spread wheat germ and sunflower seeds on a cookie sheet. Bake at 350° for 15 minutes, stirring every 5 minutes.

b. Place toasted wheat germ and sunflower seeds in a bowl.

c. Add all other ingredients except sesame seeds. Mix well.

d. Form into balls, using 1 teaspoonful of dough for each ball.

e. Roll balls in sesame seeds. (This step is not necessary.)

f. Chill for 3 hours.

g. Serve as a tasty, good-for-you snack or dessert.

1. What is the recipe for? _____

2. What kitchen utensils are needed? _____

3. What quantity of each ingredient is needed? _____

4. What ingredients are used in step <u>a</u>? _____

5. What should the oven temperature be? _____

6. How long should the wheat germ and sunflower seeds

   be baked? _____

7. How often should you stir the wheat germ and sunflower seeds

   while they are baking? _____

8. How much dough is needed to form each ball? _____

9. How long should the peanut butter balls be chilled before

   eating? _____

10. Which ingredient may be left out? _____

Name _____   Date _____

Alphabetical Order

> ■ **Alphabetical order** is used in many kinds of listings.
> EXAMPLE: Miss Clark's class list: Adams, Coss, Edwards, Gutierrez, Lee, Ortega, Shapiro, Turner

A. Complete each sentence below.

1. The letter n comes after _____ and before _____ .

2. The letters between s and w are _____ .

> ■ Entries in a dictionary or an encyclopedia appear in alphabetical order, according to their first letters, second letters, third letters, and so on.
> EXAMPLE: wave, wax, web, weed, wish, wisp

B. Number the words in each group in alphabetical order.

    3   4   2   1
1. whale, where, weary, water

2. school, second, safety, sailor

3. earth, ease, each, earn

4. recess, rain, ring, rose

C. Number the encyclopedia entries in each column in alphabetical order.

1. _____ Bell, Alexander Graham

2. _____ Berlin

3. _____ Bear

1. _____ Panda

2. _____ Pago Pago

3. _____ Panama Canal

> ■ Names in a telephone book are listed in alphabetical order, according to last names. When several people have the same last name, their names are arranged in alphabetical order, according to first names.   EXAMPLE: Barnes, John; Barnes, William; Barton, Clyde; Barwin, James D.

D. Copy the names in the order you would find them in a telephone book.

T. C. Caskey _____

Louis J. Caskey _____

Cindy Lyons _____

Paul Lyndale _____

Dictionary: Guide Words

> ■ **Guide words** are words that appear at the top of each page in a dictionary. They show the first and last entry words on the page. Guide words tell whether an entry word is listed on that page.   EXAMPLE: **beets/beyond:** The word <u>begin</u> will appear on the page. The word <u>bid</u> will not.

A. Read each pair of guide words and the list of entry words below. Put a check in front of each entry word that would appear on the page.

1. blade/bluff

_____ blur   _____ blast

_____ blink   _____ black

_____ blame   _____ blaze

_____ blossom   _____ blunder

_____ blush   _____ blouse

2. intend/island

_____ into   _____ invent

_____ instrument   _____ isn't

_____ introduce   _____ irrigate

_____ iron   _____ itch

_____ inward   _____ invite

B. Read each pair of guide words and the list of entry words below. Circle only the entry words that would appear on the page. Then write those words in the order in which they would appear in the dictionary.

1. meal/minister

meanwhile _____

melody _____

meadow _____

mention _____

mischief _____

2. product/provide

professor _____

propeller _____

proceed _____

program _____

protest _____

3. rear/rescue

recess _____

realize _____

recognize _____

reckon _____

receive _____

4. miserable/mitten

mist _____

mischief _____

miss _____

mite _____

mixture _____

Dictionary: Syllables

> - A **syllable** is each part of a word that is pronounced at one time.
> - Dictionary entry words are divided into syllables to show how to divide a word at the end of a writing line.
> - Put a **hyphen** (-) between syllables when dividing a word.
>   EXAMPLE: a-wak-en

- **Find each word in a dictionary. Write the word, placing a hyphen between syllables.**

1. chemical ___chem-i-cal___
2. gasoline _____
3. degree _____
4. marvelous _____
5. disappear _____
6. chimney _____
7. continent _____
8. miserable _____
9. generally _____
10. glacier _____
11. arithmetic _____
12. exercise _____
13. hospital _____
14. problem _____
15. window _____
16. language _____
17. agriculture _____
18. parakeet _____
19. beginning _____
20. simple _____

21. determine _____
22. musician _____
23. salary _____
24. cheetah _____
25. interrupt _____
26. dentist _____
27. recognize _____
28. rascal _____
29. innocent _____
30. educate _____
31. achievement _____
32. darling _____
33. homestead _____
34. calendar _____
35. missionary _____
36. farewell _____
37. aluminum _____
38. bacteria _____
39. program _____
40. banana _____

Using an Encyclopedia

- An **encyclopedia** is a reference book that has articles on many different subjects. The articles are arranged in alphabetical order in different books, called volumes. Each volume is marked to show which subjects are inside.
- **Guide words** are used to show the first subject on each page.
- There is a listing of **cross-references** at the end of most articles to related subjects that the reader can use to get more information on that subject.

A. Read the sample encyclopedia entry below. Use it to answer the questions that follow.

WATER is a liquid. Like air (oxygen), water is necessary for all living things. A person can live only a few days without water. Water is lost from the body every day and must be replaced. Drinking and eating replace water. About 60 percent of a person's body weight is water. *See also* OXYGEN.

1. What is the article about? _____

2. Why is water important? _____

3. How much of a person's body is water? _____

4. How is water in the body replaced? _____

5. What other subject could you look under to get more information? _____

6. What could be another related topic? _____

OXYGEN is a gas that has no smell, no taste, and no color. Nearly all living things need oxygen to live. Oxygen mixes with other things in a person's body to produce energy needed for life processes. Oxygen is also an important part of water. Oxygen is sometimes called air.

7. How are oxygen and water the same? _____

8. Does the above cross-reference mention water? _____

9. How does the article describe oxygen? _____

10. What is another word for oxygen? _____

- When looking for an article in the encyclopedia:
  Look up the last name of a person.
    EXAMPLE: To find an article on Babe Ruth, look under <u>Ruth</u>.
  Look up the first word in the name of a city, state, or country.
    EXAMPLE: To find an article on New York City, look under
    <u>New</u>.
  Look up the most important word in the name of a general
  topic.
    EXAMPLE: To find an article on the brown bear, look under
    <u>bear</u>.

B. **Write the word you would look under to find an article on each of the following subjects.**

1. Susan B. Anthony _____

2. salt water _____

3. New Mexico _____

4. lakes in Scotland _____

5. Rio de Janeiro _____

6. United Kingdom _____

7. modern literature _____

8. breeds of horses _____

C. **The example below shows how the volumes of one encyclopedia are marked. The volumes are numbered. The subjects are in alphabetical order. Write the number of the volume in which you would find each article.**

A	B	C-CH	CI-CZ	D	E	F	G	H	I-J	K
1	2	3	4	5	6	7	8	9	10	11

L	M	N	O	P	Q-R	S	T	U-V	W-Z
12	13	14	15	16	17	18	19	20	21

_____ 1. caring for chickens

_____ 2. the flag of the United States

_____ 3. how glass is made

_____ 4. vitamins

_____ 5. reptiles

_____ 6. the history of Japan

_____ 7. how rainbows are formed

_____ 8. pine trees

Unit 6 Test

Choose the correct answer to each question.

1. Which of the following steps would come first?

   A ○ Apply second coat of paint.

   B ○ Scrape away old, flaky paint.

   C ○ Apply paint with smooth, even strokes

   D ○ Stir paint well.

2. Which would you do after mixing all ingredients together?

   A ○ Put in microwave-safe dish.

   B ○ Stir well and put back in microwave for 10 minutes.

   C ○ Set timer for 20 minutes.

   D ○ Start microwave oven.

Which group of words is in alphabetical order?

3. **A** ○ pair   **B** ○ germ   **C** ○ quake   **D** ○ seal
   pear   gear   quest   search
   part   gem   quiver   section
   page   gelatin   quick   serve

4. **A** ○ dog   **B** ○ back   **C** ○ scamp   **D** ○ pert
   doing   bacteria   scan   peeve
   dwindle   bagful   scare   pester
   dwell   bagel   scat   person

Which word would be on the same page as the guide words?

5. **card / case**

   A ○ capital   **C** ○ carrot

   B ○ cabin   **D** ○ cast

6. **vacate / vain**

   A ○ valentine   **C** ○ van

   B ○ vacant   **D** ○ vacation

Which shows the correct division of the word into syllables?

7. **carefully**

   A ○ ca-re-fu-lly

   B ○ care-ful-ly

   C ○ care-full-y

   D ○ care-fu-lly

8. **forgotten**

   A ○ for-got-ten

   B ○ for-gotten

   C ○ for-go-tten

   D ○ for-go-tt-en

9. **skyscraper**

   A ○ sk-yscra-per

   B ○ sky-scra-per

   C ○ sky-scrap-er

   D ○ sky-scrape-r

10. **beautiful**

   A ○ bea-u-ti-ful

   B ○ beaut-i-ful

   C ○ be-au-ti-ful

   D ○ beau-ti-ful

Name _____ Date _____

Choose the correct answer to each question.

11. Which is not part of an encyclopedia?

A ○ guide words

B ○ dictionary

C ○ volumes

D ○ subjects in alphabetical order

12. In which volume would *the importance of the water cycle* be found?

A ○ C

B ○ T

C ○ W

D ○ I

Use the sample encyclopedia article to answer the questions.

BRAN Bran is the outer layers of food grains. When flour is made, the outer layers of grain come off. These particles are bran. Bran is a very healthful food. It is full of vitamins and minerals. Bran is used as a breakfast food and as an ingredient in baking. Pure bran is dark brown in color. Pure bran is often combined with other cereal grains, such as wheat. *See also* FIBER and CEREAL.

13. What is the article about?

A ○ flour

B ○ grains

C ○ vitamins

D ○ bran

14. What is bran?

A ○ outer particles of grain

B ○ flour

C ○ wheat

D ○ a color

15. How is bran obtained?

A ○ by taking off the outer layers of grains

B ○ by baking grains

C ○ by combining grains

D ○ by coloring grains

16. What are the cross–references?

A ○ flour and grain

B ○ fiber and cereal

C ○ vitamins and minerals

D ○ cereal and wheat

Choose the volume in an encyclopedia where each article would be found.

A–C	D–F	G–I	J–L	M–N	O–Q	R–S	T–V	W–Z
1	2	3	4	5	6	7	8	9

17. the city of Springfield

A ○ 1   C ○ 7

B ○ 6   D ○ 8

18. Walt Disney

A ○ 1   C ○ 8

B ○ 2   D ○ 9

Answer Key

Assessment Test (Pages 8–11)
A. 1. S **2.** H **3.** A **4.** H
B. ball
C. 1. C **2.** P **3.** S **4.** C
D. 1. will not **2.** he will
E. The words in bold should be circled.
   1. E, **days,** are **2.** IN, **you,** do mean **3.** D, **I,** like
   4. IM, **You,** should take
F. 1. CS **2.** CP
G. 1. RO **2.** CS
H. Underline: dog, park. Circle: José, Rachel
I. car's
J. 1. H **2.** L **3.** A
K. 1. future **2.** past **3.** present
L. 1. Did, see **2.** drank, broke **3.** written, sung
   4. ate, began
M. 1. PP **2.** SP **3.** OP
N. 1. adjective **2.** adverb
O. The words in bold should be circled.
   An oil spot was **on** the floor **of** the garage.
P. 1. Teach **2.** good **3.** set **4.** sit **5.** may
Q.
                 487 E. Deer Run
                 Sacramento, CA 94099
                 Feb. 27, 19___

Dear Luke,
   What's it like living in California? I can't even imagine it. The postcards you sent were fantastic! It will be fun to come and visit. I'm worried about earthquakes, though.
   Take care of yourself.
                 Your friend,
                 Paul

R. and S. Answers will vary.
T. 1. 3 **2.** 1 **3.** 2
U. 1. slum-ber **2.** smat-ter-ing **3.** slug-gish
V. 1. locks **2.** help ships move through canals **3.** two
   4. stairs **5.** canal
W. Students should circle the words in bold.
   1. 5, **mining 2.** 7, **Twain 3.** 5, **Nile**
   4. 7, **tundra 5.** 7, **Sweden 6.** 3, **Great 7.** 3, **gardens**
   8. 8, **volcanoes**

Unit 1: Vocabulary
Synonyms (P. 13)
Answers will vary.
Antonyms (P. 14)
A. Suggested antonyms:
   1. light **2.** lazy **3.** down **4.** quiet **5.** south **6.** sell
   7. night **8.** sweet **9.** go **10.** bad **11.** large **12.** smooth
   13. white **14.** below **15.** smiling **16.** over **17.** ugly
   18. hot **19.** weak **20.** narrow **21.** happy **22.** west
   23. warm **24.** start **25.** light **26.** short **27.** take
   28. easy
B. Antonyms will vary.
Homonyms (P. 15)
A. Phrase content will vary. Suggested homonyms:
   1. hall **2.** rode **3.** some **4.** weigh **5.** knew **6.** meet

B. 1. too, to **2.** two **3.** to, two, too **4.** to, two, to
C. 1. there, their **2.** They're, their **3.** They're, their
Homographs (P. 16)
A. 1. b **2.** b **3.** a **4.** b **5.** b
B. 1. snap **2.** limp **3.** row **4.** bark **5.** squash
C. Sentences will vary.
Prefixes and Suffixes (P. 17)
A. 1. kindness, the state of being kind **2.** predate, to date before **3.** helpless, without help **4.** remade, made again
B. 1. relives **2.** endless **3.** darkness **4.** predawn
   5. misread **6.** delightful
Contractions (P. 18)
A. 1. who's **2.** couldn't **3.** they've **4.** I'll **5.** doesn't
   6. should've **7.** you'd **8.** I've **9.** that's **10.** didn't
   11. let's **12.** they're
B. 1. wasn't **2.** Where's **3.** She's **4.** I've **5.** can't
   6. What'll **7.** Let's **8.** he'll **9.** What's **10.** it's
   11. I'm or it's **12.** couldn't
Compound Words (P. 19)
A. 1. high/way **2.** old/time **3.** full/moon **4.** snow/flake
   5. air/conditioner **6.** fire/drill **7.** bare/foot **8.** baby/sitter
   9. splash/down **10.** sweat/shirt **11.** high/rise
   12. earth/quake **13.** half/mast **14.** bull/dog
   15. skate/board
B. 1. hardware or neighborhood **2.** backyard or neighborhood **3.** afternoon **4.** outcome
   5. neighborhood
C. 1. houseboat, boathouse **2.** cupcake, cakewalk
Unit 1 TEST, Pages 20–21
1. C **2.** A **3.** B **4.** C **5.** D **6.** B **7.** D **8.** A **9.** B **10.** C
11. C **12.** B **13.** D **14.** C **15.** D **16.** D **17.** C **18.** A **19.** D
20. C **21.** D **22.** A **23.** C **24.** B **25.** B **26.** C **27.** B **28.** D
29. A **30.** B

Unit 2: Sentences
Recognizing Sentences (P. 22)
A. *S* should precede the following sentences:
   3, 6, 7, 9, 10, 12, 13, 15, 17
B. Sentences will vary.
Types of Sentences (P. 23)
A. 1. interrogative **2.** declarative **3.** interrogative
   4. declarative **5.** declarative **6.** interrogative
   7. interrogative **8.** declarative
B. Sentences and labels will vary.
More Types of Sentences (P. 24)
A. 1. imperative **2.** exclamatory **3.** imperative
   4. imperative **5.** exclamatory **6.** imperative
   7. exclamatory **8.** exclamatory **9.** imperative
   10. imperative **11.** exclamatory **12.** imperative
   13. imperative **14.** exclamatory
B. Sentences will vary.
Complete Subjects and Predicates (P. 25)
A. 1. S **2.** P **3.** P **4.** S **5.** S **6.** P
B. Subjects and predicates will vary.

Simple Subjects (P. 26)
A. Students should circle the words in bold.
1. Freshly-picked **morels**/are . . .
2. These **mushrooms**/can . . .
3. A rich **soil**/is . . .
4. Grassy **spots**/are . . .
5. The **spring**/must . . .
6. Damp **earth**/is . . .
7. A clear, sunny **sky**/means . . .
8. **We**/never . . .
9. Tall, wet **grasses**/often . . .
10. **We**/must . . .
11. These spongy little **mushrooms**/do . . .
12. **You**/might . . .

B. Sentences will vary.

Simple Predicates (P. 27)
A. Students should circle the words in bold.
1. Many tourists/**visit** the Netherlands in April or May.
2. The beautiful tulip blooms/**reach** their height of glory during these months.
3. Visitors/**can see** flowers for miles and miles.
4. Joan/**is dreaming** of a trip to the Netherlands someday.
5. She/**has seen** colorful pictures of tulips in catalogs.
6. The catalogs/**show** tulips of all colors in full bloom.
7. Joan/**is** anxious to see the tulips herself.
8. Passing travelers/**can buy** large bunches of flowers.
9. Every Dutch city/**has** flowers everywhere.
10. Flower vases/**can be found** in the cars of some Dutch people.

B. Predicates will vary.
C. Sentences will vary.

Understood Subjects (P. 28)
A. 1. (You) Turn 2. (You) turn 3. (You) Park 4. (You) Do block 5. (You) Leave 6. (You) Help 7. (You) Hold 8. (You) Get 9. (You) Lock 10. (You) Check 11. (You) Knock 12. (You) Try

B. Sentences will vary.

Using Compound Subjects (P. 29)
A. 1. C, Paul Bunyan and Babe
2. Babe
3. C, Maine and Minnesota
4. Babe
5. C, Lumberjacks and storytellers

B. 1. Tennessee and Texas claim Davy Crockett as their hero.
2. Great bravery and unusual skills made Davy Crockett famous.
3. True stories and tall tales about Davy Crockett were passed down.
4. These true stories and tall tales made Davy Crockett a legend.

C. Sentences will vary.

Using Compound Predicates (P. 30)
A. 1. C, wrote and printed its own newspaper.
2. was named editor-in-chief.
3. C, assigned the stories and approved the final copies.
4. were reporters.
5. C, wrote the news stories or edited the stories.
6. C, interviewed a new student and wrote up the interview.

B. Sentences may vary. Suggested:
1. Jenny covered the baseball game and described the best plays.
2. Sue and Kim wrote jokes and made up puzzles.
3. Luis corrected the news stories and wrote headlines.
4. Alex typed the newspaper but couldn't print it.

C. Sentences will vary.

Simple and Compound Sentences (P. 31)
A. 1. S, George Washington/witnessed
2. C, John Adams/was his son/was
3. S, Thomas Jefferson/was
4. C, The British/burned President Madison/escaped

B. Sentences may vary. Suggested:
1. Andrew Jackson was called "Old Hickory," and Zachary Taylor's nickname was "Old Rough and Ready."
2. Four presidents had no children, but John Tyler had fourteen children.
3. Chester A. Arthur put the first bathroom in the White House, and Benjamin Harrison put in electric lights.
4. Woodrow Wilson coached college football, and Ronald Reagan announced baseball games on radio.

Correcting Run-on Sentences (P. 32)
A. 1. marsupials. All 2. marsupial. The 3. kangaroos. They . . . kangaroos. Some 4. Australia. Their

B. Mexico. They
white. They
teeth. The
babies. Each

Unit 2 TEST, Pages 33–34
1. B 2. D 3. B 4. A 5. C 6. D 7. D 8. C 9. B 10. A 11. A 12. D 13. A 14. B   15. C 16. C 17. B 18. A

Unit 3: Grammar and Usage
Nouns (P. 35)
A. Nouns will vary.
B. 1. section, United States, scenes, beauty 2. trees, California, giants, forest 3. fall, tourists, trees, Vermont 4. cities, beaches 5. flowers, grasses, prairies, Texas 6. Montana, Wyoming, mountains 7. citizens, state, pride, charm, state

Common and Proper Nouns (P. 36)
A. Proper nouns will vary.
B. Common nouns will vary.

Singular and Plural Nouns (P. 37)
A. 1. P, boot 2. S, armies 3. S, matches 4. P, map 5. P, inch 6. S, feet 7. S, heroes 8. S, alleys 9. S, babies 10. P, woman 11. P, half 12. P, sky 13. S, wives 14. P, box 15. S, beaches 16. S, books

B. 1. stories 2. watches 3. players 4. shelves 5. monkeys 6. children

Answer Key
© Steck-Vaughn Publishing Company

94

Language Practice 5, SV 7161-9